EATENONHA

EATENONHA

Native Roots of Modern Democracy

GEORGES SIOUI

McGill-Queen's University Press
Montreal & Kingston • London • Chicago

© McGill-Queen's University Press 2019

ISBN 978-0-7735-5639-3 (cloth)
ISBN 978-0-2280-0046-4 (ePDF)
ISBN 978-0-2280-0047-1 (ePUB)

Legal deposit third quarter 2019
Bibliothèque nationale du Quebec

Printed in Canada on acid-free paper that is 100% ancient forest free
(100% post-consumer recycled), processed chlorine free

Funded by the Government of Canada   Financé par le gouvernement du Canada      Canada Council for the Arts   Conseil des arts du Canada

We acknowledge the support of the Canada Council for the Arts.
Nous remercions le Conseil des arts du Canada de son soutien.

The cover image is in fond remembrance of a very dear Ojibway friend I once had in my life, Roy Thomas. At the centre: the mother giving thanks for life, teacher of the essential virtues that help create balance in society: kindness, rectitude, empathy, love, and compassion for all beings of all orders.

Library and Archives Canada Cataloguing in Publication

Title: Eatenonha : native roots of modern democracy / Georges Sioui.
Names: Sioui, Georges E., 1948– author.
Description: Includes bibliographical references.
Identifiers: Canadiana (print) 20190118482 | Canadiana (ebook) 20190118504
  | ISBN 9780773556393 (hardcover) | ISBN 9780228000464 (ePDF) | ISBN
  9780228000471 (ePUB)
Subjects: LCSH: Wyandot Indians—Canada.
Classification: LCC E99.H9 S56 2019 | DDC 971.004/97555—dc23

This book was typeset in 10.5/13 Sabon.

CONTENTS

PREFACE

This is a story of me, of my Seawi Clan, and of my Wendat people. It is also a story of Canada and, as such, is an exploration into the historical and future significance of the Native soul of Canada in the world context. Most centrally, it presents our country, Canada, as our motherland, our *Eatenonha*, instead of as a common property we acquire and own by the fact of being and becoming Canadian. This book is also a gift, from me and from my people, to Canada and to the world.

In the first chapter, I am inviting you, dear friend and reader, on a road trip in the eastern United States that I made with my very dear life-companion Bárbara in February 2012, where she and I converse, and at times surmise, about some less certain, sparsely documented aspects of my people's historical trajectory. This first section also takes you to Brazil and Argentina to give you a glimpse into my people's ancestral thinking about the continental unity of a Native American way of comprehending life and the world.

In chapter 2, I take you back, through a tale of my unconventional family's life on our Reserve, to a time when Nature herself was so much more present than now in our ways of thinking and living. That piece is titled "Seawi: Hurons of the Rising Sun."

Chapter 3 presents the virtually unknown history of the Seawi, a group of Wendat traditionally refractory to the socio-political order imposed by the colonial powers of New France. That section begins to explain how an ancient Aboriginal sense of Canada's history was preserved among that community. The section also contains two lectures I gave, one in Innsbruck, Austria, in 2010 and the other in Saskatoon, Saskatchewan, in 2013. In these two papers, I present some of the life, ideology, and work of my own parents to further familiarize you, my reader, with the social and family context where I have my roots.

Chapter 4, "The *Sioui* Case Explained," is my rendering of how this landmark legal case was founded and engineered to be victorious in the Supreme Court of Canada in 1990. It is meant as an illustration of how my people's preservation of an ancestral sense of our (and Canada's) history and evolution was used to create a case where all components of the larger society saw how we collectively stood to come out winning, mostly through gaining a new capacity to achieve a more unified, stronger society.

Chapter 5, "The Essential Thread of Canada's History," constitutes an original retelling of how a large body of Native nations in the Northeast had created, in pre-European times, what I style a "commonwealth of nations" based on peace, trade, and reciprocity. The geopolitical centre of this vast commercial and social network was the Wendat Confederacy. Contrary to what is still taught in almost all Canadian schools, the Five Nations (Iroquois) Confederacy, in Aboriginal times, only occupied a place of marginal importance. It was not able to, nor did it have a will to, threaten or disrupt the centuries-old political order established in the land – a role and an ambition that have conventionally and unjustly been ascribed to the Hodenosaunee (the Iroquois). From this novel perspective, Canada can no longer be thought of as a country fated to borrow its political ideology from its reputedly stronger and culturally more sophisticated neighbour to the south. Instead, our new understanding of the Aboriginal geopolitics of the Northeast makes us see Canada as the true originator, and potentially the international seat, of the discourse on modern democracy in times to come.

I have titled the last chapter of this essay "Eatenonha: Native Roots of Modern Democracy." My whole purpose in writing this book has been to reveal to my readers, to all Canadians, and to the world some of the deepest, most honoured secrets possessed by my people and by all people who are Indigenous, as well as those who understand and respect our Aboriginal/Indigenous way of thinking and living. To contextualize those secrets, I have chosen to write about the Wendat because they are my own people and because among Canada's many first civilizations, we were the one that most immediately and materially attended to the birth and the beginnings of Canada as it is now known.

The most important, most ineffable secret I have been meaning to share with all of you, dear readers, is that we, First Peoples, had created for ourselves a society, indeed a world, that can be looked at as a true democracy. A society where all beings of all natures are equally valued and respected and where women – and the feminine order – are meant and made to have their place in the centre of their families and communities. What I have proposed in this essay is, quite simply, that our world can only achieve its due measure of order, peace, and security if we, collectively, strive to re-educate ourselves with regard to the place that the Great Power of the Universe, the Supreme Being, or still, Nature herself, has willed us to occupy as humans amid the Great Sacred Circle of Life. Man, the leader, the defender, the provider, can only accomplish the roles flowing from his own nature if he does not substitute himself for the woman and usurp her place in the centre. This is what is essentially implied by the term *matricentrism*.

In my life, I have been instructed by my Elders to "help heal the world." The present book represents my – and my people's – continuing quest to carry out that duty, in unity with the whole human and other-than-human community. Together, my dear readers and relatives, we will keep on creating a great, world-wide way of educating all of our peoples, all our children. I, and countless others, have been building and promoting this virtual institution for many years: The School of Circular and Matricentric Thinking.

Etsagon, my dear relatives! (Let us take heart and be happy!)

ACKNOWLEDGEMENTS

I dedicate this book most tenderly to my parents, Georges-Albert and Éléonore; to my so beloved wife Bárbara, the Hawk Spirit Woman who is the constant guardian creating the conditions without which my own creations would never materialize; and to my son, Miguel Paul Sastaretsi, a true Spirit-Warrior who walks with respect and pride on the sacred, immemorial path of our Wendat ancestors. I also dedicate this lovingly to my Seawi Clan; fraternally, to my Huron-Wendat Nation; fondly, to all my Indian, Métis, and Inuit friends and relatives among whom, through the years, I have known some of the best, sweetest times of my life – I especially wish to mention three names: Herb Nabigon and Leo Yerxa, my very dear Ojibway neechees, both recently gone on to the spirit world, and my equally great and dear Mohawk friend and teacher Rarihokwats; heartily, to every citizen of all our Indigenous nations of the "Four Americas." To all of you, our youth, of all origins: May you find and keep your "Indian heart" – you have (!) to stay and show the world a new way; to all of you, my human brothers and sisters of everywhere – I love you, there is no distance between us, you are my family! To the University of Ottawa, who has treated me and our Aboriginal Peoples with respect and an open, caring mind; to my colleagues of our Departments of Classics and Religious Studies, of History, and of the Institute of Canadian and Aboriginal Studies. I especially greet my very dear Canadian-Italian brother and special colleague Pierluigi Piovanelli; my sister

Marie-Françoise Guédon, a truly great thinker of the Circle; my old friend and comrade-in-arms Chad Gaffield; my fellow-historian and brother Pierre Anetili; and my long-time friend and fellow-philosopher and emerging novelist Michel Gardaz. I also wish to salute warmly John Beckwith and David Fallis, two great musicians of the University of Toronto, who helped me discover myself and being discovered as a songwriter and musician. I thank and greet my friends of McGill-Queen's University Press: my long-time friend and brother Philip Cercone and his excellent, ever so helpful team who put their best personal effort and also their enthusiasm and joy into creating this second (truly beautiful) book of mine to come out at MQUP. I would not want to forget to thank wholeheartedly a superb editor, now my friend, Kaitlin Littlechild and her three young children who have had to be extra-patient to allow their mother to achieve a work of such high quality. Finally, to our common mother Eatenonha and to the Creator of all things, the one we call the Great Spirit, Great Mystery, or, as our Wendat forebears used to conceive of Her/Him, Aronia, "the Sky."

A NOTE ON TERMINOLOGY

I use several words when writing about Aboriginal Peoples. Here is some explanation for this terminology.

ABORIGINAL This is the official appellation when one wants to include all three "branches" of the Aboriginal Peoples recognized by Canada, that is, the Inuit, the Métis, and the First Nations. However, one needs to be aware that many, if not all the citizens belonging to these three distinct peoples, do not choose to refer to themselves as "Aboriginal." Instead, they think of themselves as members of the Inuit, the Métis, or the First Nations. In the case of the latter, most members of those nations prefer to refer to themselves by using the name of their nation: I am Cree, Siksika, Mi'kmaq, Kootenay, and so forth.

AMERINDIAN That term, obviously made up of the words "America" and "Indian," is meant to safeguard the ever-important vocable "Indian" while indicating that one is referring to the "Indians" of America, not to the people of India. It is used more frequently in the francophone context of Quebec.

FIRST PEOPLES This expression may at times be preferred to "First Nations," which does have an overtone of governmental approval.

INDIAN Despite the historical error it constantly exposes, this term remains a frequent choice by many First Nations people to designate who and what they are. The nations who have a Treaty relationship with Canada (the British Crown) hold that word as somewhat sacred because that is the word inscribed in their Treaty and because the wording of those Treaties is never to be changed in any way whatsoever.

INDIGENOUS This is the name to use when thinking and speaking of "Aboriginal" peoples on an international scale.

NATIVE I use this word interchangeably with any of the other terms mentioned above. It is the one used in the title of my book because it is at once the most neutral and the most inclusive designation of all.

EATENONHA

INTRODUCTION

My essential purpose in writing this essay is to offer a Native understanding of the history and of the deeper nature of the wonderful country named Canada. In the traditional manner that I have learned from my Huron people, my deeper intent is to offer a remedy for the soul of my many fellow Canadians who go about feeling that they miss having a sense of the history and of the "real" nature of the country they have grown to love for her utter beauty and bounty but have never been duly taught how to preserve and venerate as their motherland in return. On another level, I have often heard, mostly by fellow Canadians, that our dear country has historically misunderstood, and still misunderstands, the way to acquire long-lasting respectability in the eyes of other nations and achieve the desired and deserved global stature. The real way is to give recognition to the Aboriginal civilizations that gave it birth and being and provide it with its vital cultural and spiritual inspiration – that is, the civilizations elaborated over untold centuries by the peoples native to the soil of this land. I, of course, share that feeling of regret about the way my people and my land are wasted away through the systemic maintenance of old, maladapted, imported, life-corroding ideologies.

The word *Canada* is derived from our own Native word *Kanatha*, meaning "the Chief-town," or "the big village," and comes from one of our ancestral languages once spoken in the region of Stadacona (now Quebec City). The Wendat word in the title of this essay, *Eatenonha*, represents a concept found in many of our ancestral languages that expresses a traditional attitude of love, faith, and respect toward the Earth, our common Mother, and toward everything feminine in nature.

Although my aim is to enable my fellow Canadians to understand and relate better to the physical being and spirit of our Earth Mother, another goal I pursue with even more fervour is to succeed in expressing ideas that originate from my people's thinking in a way that may interest and positively inspire our brothers and sisters from everywhere. Deepak Chopra, the rightly celebrated Indo-American physician and spiritualist, has written: "Our collective future depends on opening channels of compassion, acceptance, and understanding of others." My wish is to see included in the word "others" not only us humans, but all the beings that make up, with us, the Great Sacred Circle of Life.

Renowned Kenyan scientist, environmental activist, and Nobel Peace Prize laureate Wangari Maathai teaches a touching lesson in her beautiful and famous allegory of the hummingbird. The whole forest was on fire and the animals, frightened and infinitely sad, helplessly stood and watched it burn. The tiniest of them all, the hummingbird, said to herself that she was going to do something and, who knows, maybe others would also want to try to help save their dear forest, their "Mother." The tiny hummingbird undertook to transport in her mouth minute droplets of water from a hidden spring and launch them on the conflagration from up high.

Other animals, powerful and imposing, such as the elephant who could have fetched much more water and thrown it on the fire with her big trunk, only worsened the general state of panic when they loudly proclaimed with a tone of wisdom that rang false that there was nothing left to do but helplessly watch the planet go down the drain. Our great African sister urges us all to be a hummingbird, to do what we can to help the community! (Even if what you do seems or is deemed unimportant.)

My maternal family has been known for its healers, men and women. "We have to help heal the world," I have often heard my grandmother, Caroline, and my mother, Éléonore, say. Seven words that, I soon enough understood, contain the whole social and educational philosophy of our Aboriginal nation not so long ago happy, strong, and prosperous, and almost destroyed in the process of colonial invasion. Despite the contempt and violence that have come upon us, we can continue to find peace and balance instead of the sterile and pernicious feeling of being powerless victims. We must cultivate our new generations' faith in the wisdom of the ancestors – a wisdom that is the result of an immemorial relation of respect, trust, and affection for our common Mother Earth, our Eatenonha. Following the teachings and the living example of our sages, such as Caroline, Éléonore, Deepak, and Wangari, we all must make the most of the mental and spiritual gifts and of the knowledge of our respective forefathers and foremothers to help one another, all of us, heal the world.

Kiowa-Cherokee poet, painter, and novelist Norman Scott Momaday, Pulitzer Prize winner for his novel *The House Made of Dawn* (1969), writes that humans are made of words and are the story of themselves. Some Indians say that humans were created by The Great Spirit because He/She loves stories. Following this Indigenous way of thinking and telling, this essay will have the form and the consistency of a story. It will be the yet unknown story of my family, of our Wendat Nation (renamed *Huron* by the French), of our central place and role in relation to our neighbours, and of the kind of world we have assisted one another in creating over so many centuries.

My book will, in fact, be my and my people's rendition of what has truly happened to us, as native people of this land. It is how we feel that a non-Indigenous account of our history has harmed and continues to harm us, Indigenous Peoples, our land, and therefore, the chances of all people, human and other-than-human, of continuing to have a happy and secure life here, in this land named Canada that we all inhabit together. This book is an invitation to you, all my relatives and friends, to think, in the spirit of Canada's and America's first civilizations, about why we must and how we are to create a truly strong and unified country where we can all feel included, valued, and celebrated for the wonderful, beautiful diversity we bring to it – a Canada that is first and foremost our Mother Earth, a Canada we will think of as our Eatenonha, our beloved motherland.

In writing this book, I also pursue a goal regarding our whole human community, at the spiritual level. It is about a prediction made by many of our sages of old, even before the arrival of Europeans among us. These ancient Elders foresaw an initial time of intense assault against and destruction of their cultures and peoples through the presence of newcomers and an immense demographic void produced through said invasion. But they also saw that there would come a time when the descendants of the original newcomers, along with the other peoples of the world, would see the need for creating in their midst a place for America's ancient thinking ways and wisdom. As time has gone by, our sages have wanted to leave with the evolving world the teaching that, in this present age where borders between cultures and societies are losing importance and often are erased, their American continent has become the scene where all of humanity is to become unified. This, the sages have thought all through this age of destruction and progressive global unification, is going to be effected through a spiritual vision that is essential to the whole American continent. This simple vision is that all life is a sacred circle of interdependent relations and that failure by humans to recognize and respect that reality would cause the end of human existence in our beautiful, wonderful home – our Mother Earth, our Eatenonha.

Following the tenet that has come down to me and to my people from many of our Elders, of I would say all our Native American Nations, I posit that the circular, Earth-centred cosmology that is the philosophical mark of a great many, if not all, Aboriginal Peoples of our continent represents a vitally important source of concepts and ideas for the spiritual renewal of a world torn between conflicting moral and religious values. Over recent decades, our global society has felt an increasing threat to its peace and stability because of a widening divide between several of the world's great religions. Thinkers on all sides of this divide are often heard expressing the idea that there is a great, historic opportunity for all sides to rebalance their ways of viewing and living their respective spirituality, thereby helping to solve this ever more destructive crisis that impoverishes our world and the world of all our yet unborn children. For, if we are all universally condemned to mounting misery, hunger, and death through our common, seemingly unresolvable insensitivity to the things and the beings that are the very sources of our physical, intellectual, emotional, and spiritual lives, we will certainly and soon enough all go down fighting one another. As to us, First Peoples of our continent, we consider that we have known and suffered enough through the religious and ideological fanaticism brought to our lands by different peoples. Our plea to the world is that it be attentive to the vision that we propose for our common future security and well-being. It is not a new vision, in fact, it is ancestral to all human societies: it is the vision of the Great Sacred Circle of Life. It is all about how and why we must love and respect our Mother Earth, our Eatenonha.

I humbly, earnestly, and wholeheartedly propose to all my brothers and sisters of all peoples that, with open hearts and minds and in a spirit of universal inclusiveness, we begin to seek out and listen to the essential spiritual messages of those who at times are called "the fourth family of nations (or peoples)."[1] The First Peoples of America and, by extension, all the Indigenous peoples of the world all speak and understand the same spiritual language, the language of the sacred web of universal relations uniting all beings, the language of our respective motherlands and our common Mother Earth.

CHAPTER ONE

A ROAD TRIP IN THE EASTERN
UNITED STATES

SYRACUSE, NEW YORK, 26 FEBRUARY 2012

I am an off-Reserve Indian (an Indian who lives outside of his Reserve). My home is in Gatineau, Quebec. Our immediate family consists of my wife Bárbara, our son Miguel Paul, and me. Both of my parents have now gone on to the spirit world and most of my blood relatives still live on our home Reserve of Wendake (or Village-des-Hurons), situated fifteen kilometres north of the city of Quebec.

I am an Indian "through and through," as my grandmother Caroline, a much-respected healer, sententiously informed an older French-Canadian friend and patient who, judging only on my "un-Indian" looks, had deeply hurt the feelings of her seven-year-old first grandson. Besides, having been raised around four Huron grandparents, what else could I possibly be but a Huron Indian, despite my looks? But that is quite a long story and it is, in good part, the one that this book is going to recount.

My wife and I have been gone for eighteen days on a road trip to the eastern United States and have covered 5,300 kilometres (3,500 miles) so far. Quite unlike the past few days, coming through Kentucky, Ohio, Pennsylvania, and eastern New York, today will be a mild, sunshiny, spring-like day, and the quaint, quiet country roads of upstate New York will see us back to the Canadian border in a matter of about four hours.

We wake up at around eight o'clock and stay each in our bed for a while, taking time to enjoy this cozy and tranquil final abode on our trip. I am thinking of the many places we have seen. It has been a voyage through space as well as through time: we left home in our winter clothes and ended up in summer ones when, four days later, we got to our final destination of Miami.

Miami is where we met, in October of 1985. *Coup de foudre*, on my part. It had not been easy for either of us to communicate, each in a language unknown to the other, but later that evening we exchanged our addresses. Before parting, with an awkward kiss left on her forehead (which, months later, she told me she had found "rather cheap"), we agreed we would write. The rest, as we say, is our history. Miami, *pays de mes amours*. Miami, *tierra de mis sueños*. Miami, where I met the love of my life.

When I travel by land, I am thoroughly overtaken by a feeling of love for that land of mine, my Mother. My soul connècts passionately with the trees, rocks, water, and mountains that we pass. "These are my relatives: I have to come and visit them," I recall saying to Bárbara, while gazing affectionately at some tall trees in their rosy early-spring attire, somewhere in North Carolina. I was thus explaining (of course, needlessly because she knew it) to my life-companion that we were also making this trip out of a sense of family duty that I felt.

"Do you feel at home here, *mi amor*?" I remember asking her, referring to a notion she knows I hold dear: that many Latin Americans are native to America and should not consider themselves immigrants in any part of their continent. (We speak only Spanish together.) "No," she answered. Needing to find an explanation for that answer, I easily persuaded myself that women, because they and the Earth are of the same gender, do not need to feel "at home" anywhere. It allows them to be much more practical than us men and (almost certainly, in this moment) have thoughts such as: "How could I possibly feel at home when the weather is so much less nice and warm than in the country of Colombia where I was born?" And: "These trees

may have their charm, but they can't in the least be compared
to our palm trees, our *ceibas*, and our *guaduales*."

Our son, Miguel, insisted that we really ought to include
Nashville (a city he and his buddy Maxime had visited the previous year) in our trip if we wished to discover a different, not so
expensive, and truly fun place. Miguel sincerely and caringly felt
that his good old parents needed such diversions before this wonderful, long-awaited sabbatical of mine was over, four months
from now. Also, what made Nashville worth the detour was the
presence there of a very dear friend of ours, Márcio, our professor of (Brazilian!) Portuguese who had recently been hired at
Vanderbilt University.

It turned out that we were able to spend four very pleasant
days together, discovering a friendly and quite interesting city and
attending Márcio's classes (great and fun as ever). In the evenings, we walked down Broadway, stopping at Márcio's favourite honky-tonk bars and listening to the world's best country
and western music, live and free. (We, of course, quite gratefully
put a few dollars in the empty large plastic mustard and may-
onnaise jugs when some of those often star country musicians
shyly explained to animated crowds that this was the band's only
source of income.)

We had a grand time in the town of Nashville, Tennessee. It
is there that I saw Bárbara have her first beer ever, offered by
her very dear fellow South American, Márcio, in that extremely
North American and, in its own unique way, deeply human and
warm social environment. "*Legál!*" Brazilians would exclaim.
"*Chévere!*" Colombians would shout. "*Vive Nashville! Vive le
Tennessee! Vive notre Amérique!* Long live our beautiful, beloved
America!" says proudly and merrily the Huron writing this book.

"It has been a beautiful trip, or rather, voyage," we both commented, still lying in bed. "A gift from Nature, God, the Universe,
the Great Spirit," I remember adding, after a fashion of thanksgiving we both use. I am feeling a bit hungry and think again
of our good fortune that a plentiful, delicious, free breakfast is
awaiting us, any time until 11:00 a.m., in this huge, well-popu-
lated Embassy Suites Hotel, which is so pleasantly alive at this

moment with dozens of families out on a weekend vacation during spring break.

BRAZIL: ANOTHER AMERICA

In my book *Histories of Kanatha*, I have suggested that the world might benefit from the idea that the First Nations of the Americas look at their continent as a living entity, in fact, a very real Mother that humans do not have the right to divide into separate pieces to suit their own private needs and interests. In the same order of thinking, I have offered the idea that to us, First Nations of this "New World," there are four Americas; one for each of the four European languages that have taken root here on our soil and that enable us to communicate all together and continue to defend the integrity of our Mother Earth, our Eatenonha. Those languages are, of course, English, French, Portuguese, and Spanish. My readers may wish to read a presentation I made at the University of Costa Rica (San José, Costa Rica) in July 2015 (Appendix).

History has made me, a Wendat, be born and evolve in the French-speaking America. As a traditional Wendat, I view my most important possible contribution to the world and to my Canadian relatives of all origins to be the continuation of the historic work of my ancestors – extending their civilization of peace and of trade to the greatest possible number of peoples and territories. A very central proposition of this book is that by the time the Europeans arrived in their midst, the Wendat had created the most extensive, influential, prosperous, and virtually war-free civilization of trade anywhere in the northern part of the continent. That unique ideological legacy, in which a strong and prestigious country like Canada should take enormous pride, lies lost under the heap of prejudice and inaccuracies that still constitute much of the data utilized by our country to explain and understand its own history.

In line with this understanding of my ancestors' civilization and in a now globalized world context, I approach Brazil as another America – the fourth one – and I readily and enthusiastically recognize the necessity for me, and for others who share a similar vision, of learning the Portuguese language. I have, over the last few years, devoted sufficient effort toward that goal and I now consider myself fluent in that beautifully sonorous, warmly human language. *Gosto muito de falar português, bem especialmente o português do Brazil!* Since I am discussing the topic of the Four Americas, I am going to illustrate my deeply filial sentiments for my homeland America by sharing with you, dear readers, the feelings I expressed while I flew over a part of Spanish America, Argentina specifically, in August 2008. I am translating what I then wrote in Spanish in my diary:

> I feel very happy at seeing America, my continent: its rivers, its forests, its beauty, the life that humans have created here. I have the feeling of getting to know my Mother, of once again being born, that I have until now been half an orphan. Tears come to my eyes. I love my motherland, America. I am happy. I feel free. My vision is of a great centre of studies and of documentation on the thought-world of all the First Nations of America. I want to see our peoples create a great song, a universal dance of love for the Earth, our common Mother, made by our Creator for us to be happy, for us all to feel and be like one.

Morretes, Southern Brazil, 5 May 2012

Ever since that grand morning in February in that chic hotel in Syracuse, I had been waiting to find the time and the proper atmosphere to resume writing this present book, which had begun to take a more definitive form in my mind. Bárbara and I are in southern Brazil, sojourning during two weeks at a *pousada* (a country-style bed and breakfast) near a little town named Morretes, in the state of Paraná. We came to Rio de Janeiro two weeks ago to attend the Inter-American Congress on International Education. A good deal of our time since returning from our road trip in the United States had been dedicated to preparing for this long-anticipated five-week journey in Brazil – the last of three trips planned for my sabbatical.

We simply loved our stay in Rio, especially the social events in the evenings. The wonderful soul of Brazil, in all its uniquely powerful *joie de vivre*, came out in the music and the spectacles of samba and capoeira, where a large number of our 500-strong crowd of scholars and students joined in and danced. Many of us, most especially Bárbara, were simply transfixed in that magical atmosphere. Rio, we keep your gift in our hearts forever!

Today then, in this virtually pristine region of Brazil's famous Atlantic Forest (Mata Atlântica), I find my inspiration for writing my book rekindled. And I think that a bird, a small, special bird of seven colours, helped produce that magic moment. (In fact, in English it is called the seven-coloured tanager.) Its plumage has three distinct, strikingly beautiful greens; rich turquoise; a superb shade of blue; the brightest, merriest yellow-orange; and vivid, jet-black marks, most notably around the eyes.

I first saw this bird two days ago in a beautifully illustrated book kept with others in an elegant, sunny room situated above the main reception area of the *pousada*, next to an open verandah where, yesterday, I saw my first toucan! With childlike interest, I looked at all 200 (or so) species of birds featured in that book, all unimaginably beautiful. I playfully and decisively chose two as my favourite: first, the seven-coloured tanager (*saíra de sete cores*) and second, the multi-coloured cloth tanager (*saíra de lenço*).

Already moved by the utter beauty of that seven-coloured bird in that photograph, I was completely taken aback when, the next morning after finishing our breakfast outside on the balcony of our lovely cabin made of glass and fine Brazilian woods, Márcia, our maid and friend, prompted us to look at a bird that had just alighted on a branch strewn with orange-coloured flowers: "*Ja vejo o das sete cores*" (I am seeing the seven-coloured one). Not really believing what I was hearing, I quickly glanced in the direction that Márcia and Bárbara were pointing and there, in the flesh and feathers, was my dream-bird, a little smaller than our northern robins, intently looking our way with its piercing, coal-black eyes!

We are still in Morretes for a week. After a delightful walk among the banana trees and other luxuriant, colourful, often flowery trees that surround our cabin (and no, the bananas we eat in Canada do not nearly have such sweetness), I easily recaptured my thoughts left dormant in Syracuse, in February.

SYRACUSE, NEW YORK, SEPTEMBER 1948

I remember having first let my mind drift back to a time before I began breathing the air of this beautiful Planet Earth, when my mother was carrying me in her womb right here in the city of Syracuse in September 1948. After seven months of pregnancy, as had already been decided by my parents, my mother took a train back home to our Reserve, alone with my sixteen-month-old sister Carole. This was so that this second child of theirs could never be forced to join any army, as a free Indian ought to never be forced to do. I was told that my mother and father, judging from the size of my mother's belly and from the way she was carrying me, "knew" it was going to be a boy. They had no reason to take any chances anyway.

I thus imagined myself riding on a train inside my mother's exquisitely cozy womb, enjoying the best, easiest time of my life. I imagined long sweet conversations with her, my mother. Dreamily, I heard her talk to me about the Nature she, in the life we lived thereafter, taught me to love with all my senses and to respect as another mother, the mother of all mothers. Brought even closer together by the dull, endless sound of the train, I heard her stories about the animals, the birds, the rivers, the lakes, the mountains, and the changing seasons. I heard about how people must live to be happy, that is, by making one another happy (as her mother, Caroline, also said to us all so many times).

She led me to ask questions about many simple things, such as how and when we had come to be together in this way, about all the little ones being carried inside their mothers' bellies, and the already born with their secret hiding places in the woods, in the rocks, in the water, even in the sky behind the clouds. I thus got to know more about a mysterious, beautiful, powerful presence in my life – a man like me, my father. My mother told me about that wonderful being who loved me with his whole heart and who was going to be my main friend and guide through life until we reached the end of this earthly life and moved on to eternal life in the beautiful Land of Souls. I got to know about the Great Creator, master of all life and a Being of all wisdom and all perfection of which I am a part in the same way as all things and all beings that exist.

Then, in this timeless state we were in, I sang to my mother the song I took five years to compose for her after she left us. I wrote it in the language of our ancestors, which is no longer spoken and which I sometimes use, in an elemental form, to write very special songs because I believe that the spirits understand the languages of the heart of their human relatives. To this day, no one has heard this song except my closest relatives. I will write and translate it here, to begin to give my reader an idea of the person that my mother was, of how I related to her, and of how we, Wendat, believe our relatives live in the beautiful Land of Souls once they have departed from this earthly, visible world. I also wish to give you, my dear reader, an idea, however imperfect, of the beautiful sonority of one of the first languages of this part of our common motherland now named Canada:

"A SONG FOR MY MOTHER"

Ata Ondouen (Our Mother Earth)

Onne Ondouen My mother is gone
Onne Saouanon She has gone away
Aatiskenon Andahate Through the Path of Souls
Tanontakie She will not come back
Anan Saouanen Our mother is gone

Onne Ondouen My mother is gone
Onne Saouanon She has gone away
To Ieintchon Achaua She lives there yonder
To Aronia In the Skyworld
Aataentsikwe With Aataentsic (our Grandmother)

Onne Atanontakie She is gone forever
Ieintchon to Aronia She now lives in the Sky

Anan Atetsense Ihonhe My mother is healed
Araskwahixhen Ondouen She will live forever
Danstan Outsonuharihen She is happy
Stan Tesotondi Ongyande Anan No more will she be sick
Enikiokwandorate She is young and strong forever
Onnehonkwe Sakonchete They feast and dance up there
Toioti ne Wendate All together as do the Wendat
Ne Wendate We, the Wendat,
Otoronte Eondeon All together they sing
Eontonhouasey ne Ondouen They all love one another

Etsakon Ouatiskahouy They are happy and merry
Aeskwani Ongyandeh Strong fires are burning
Sakoncheta auoiti There is merriment and laughter
Okihoua Atisken There is a great Feast
De Ondouen And all are there
Washutawen Etsondenon The Souls of our Ancestors
Ouadhauhandikwe Are powerful
Otoronte Anan All are reunited
Auoindio With our Grandmother
Yoskaha ne Aronia All are rejoicing together
Chetoka Teareinta My mother also sings to Yoskaha
Danan Outsonuharihen The Master of the Universe
Tsonuharihen All is joy and serenity
Onne Auoiti Hoirihen No one has any sorrow
Ouadhauhandikwe Our mother is very well and happy
Aataentsikwe All are at the Great Feast of Aataentsic
Aronia, Anan, Aronia My mother, in the Sky

Aroniayeh In the great Village of Souls
Tichion Assonteh My mother is the Stars
Anan Atisken That light up the Night Sky
Eandahahatteh She is the great Path of Souls
(the "Milky Way")
Anan Soutenni Chichiyayeh She is the Full Moon
Anan Yokoisseh She is in the winds
Anan Yondotsireh In the clouds and in the rain

Onienta Ondeskoyeh In the icy snowstorm
And in the morning dew
Enondecha Onontouteh In the valleys and the mountains
Ata Eatenonha Our Mother, the Earth
Ononhoua Houaseh She lives in our hearts forever
Ahouantahan Eondenon Forever together
Issa Ata Ondouen You are our Earth and our Mother
Ata Ondouen Our Earth and our Mother
Ata Ondouen Our Earth and our Mother
Ata Ondouen Our Earth and our Mother

My mother and I, and Carole, made a wonderful trip back to Canada and to our Reserve, then called Indian Lorette, or Village-des-Hurons (Huron Village) – now renamed Wendake – where my father is from. It was there that I was born on a sunny Wednesday morning, 3 November, six weeks after we departed from Syracuse. My father had come back by then, ending a period of six years spent mostly in the state of New York. My father had forcibly resisted conscription in the army,[1] made compulsory "equally for Indians and Eskimos" mid-way through the Second World War.

Born into two traditional Wendat families, my father had been raised with the principle that Indians (we would say, nowadays, First Nations citizens) have paid an extremely high price, in human lives and in every way, in the white man's wars; in these very different times, they ought never to allow themselves to lose any more of their people in such a way. Besides, I have known my father, and all traditional people of our Indian nations, to hold peace as the highest ideal on this human plane. This, of course, is in sharp contradiction to the notion, so common in non-Indian society, that Indians love and seek war all the time, everywhere; that our people are inadequate as human beings and, therefore, deserve nothing more or better than the very sad fate they have known ever since the "civilized" world has arrived in this motherland of theirs, their Eatenonha.

A very kind and gentle man, worldly wise, and, by then, possessing a solid command of the English language, Georges-Albert

Sioui did not encounter much difficulty in re-establishing his little family in the post-war Canadian context. He first became a salesman in men's clothing and afterwards, in the life insurance business. However, though he excelled at those trades, my father was first an Indian and did not find fulfillment living and succeeding in the white man's world. He found his happiness when in contact with the heart of Nature, no longer as a free Huron hunter as in his grandfathers' days, but now as a hunting and fishing guide like his father, Paul Sioui. His father was a true master in all the ways of the forest and was much sought after by rich American tourists wanting to come to Canada and be guided by Huron and other Indian woodsmen. Their hunting and fishing expeditions took place in our ancestral forests where we had already long been deprived of our rights (and responsibilities) as original inhabitants, and which we could only frequent as guides (in reality, servants) for wealthy newcomers.

CROSSING THE UNITED STATES BORDER, 9 FEBRUARY 2012

Bárbara and I crossed the Canada–United States border on 9 February 2012. Contrary to the stressful, even scary experience it can be for many people on any given day, passing the border has always been for me a thrill, even a pleasure. The reasons for this are legal and ideological. First, to its credit, the United States still upholds, at least in part, the legal rights that Canadian Indians have from the Jay Treaty signed in 1794, by which Indian individuals were, and still are, not to be molested in their need to carry across the border goods and belongings that they require for their normal living activities.

Second, on the ideological level, Indian persons wishing to affirm their sovereignty as members of the original nations of America can do so in a legal, acceptable manner. Of course, due respect for persons and institutions always must be shown, in all circumstances, by the persons demanding entry in the United States.

In my own case, as in the case of many Indians of mixed origins particularly in southern Canada, there is a psychological factor at play – the physical features we present to the authorities, accustomed as they are to be able to distinguish a Native person by such facial or other "Indian" physical characteristics, and socially conditioned as they are by a host of stereotypes about Indians, so present in our society. The fact that I descend from four federally registered Huron-Wendat grandparents is simply obliterated by the reality of my looks. I can be taken for anything but an Indian, from Irish to Swede to German to English, and other "white" nationalities. (This curious cultural phenomenon has much to do with our ancestral *matricentrist* socio-political organization and will be looked at more in depth further on.)

That day, 9 February 2012, we made the stop at the border to answer the usual questions as to where we were going, why, and for how long, as well as to show our identification documents. As Canadian nationals are now required to do, Bárbara presented her Canadian passport. I, however, still go by our customary practice of showing only my card issued by the federal government, which ascertains my Indian status in Canada.

"What is your citizenship?" came the first question from the stern-looking customs officer, bending slightly toward us to find out, among other things, how many people were travelling in our car. "Canada," was my answer, and not "Canadian," which would, from a traditionalist standpoint, be an admission of subjection to a non-Native nation-state. Simultaneously, I handed him Bárbara's passport and my Indian status card. The officer's reaction was typical: "Which tribe are you with [*sic*]?" I was asked in a friendly tone. "Huron," was my answer. (We, Wendat, never expect people, even Indians, to know the real name of our people.) "Great!" the officer replied. "I used to play lacrosse and some of our players were Mohawk. They had very strong teams themselves, and still do!" The rest of the questions, and my answers, took the tone of an easy conversation: the reason of our trip, where we were headed, when we planned to come back home, and finally, a cordial "you folks enjoy your trip!"

In these thirty years or so together, Bárbara and I have crossed the border many times, and most of those times I recall noticing in her a surprise about how I suddenly showed a joyful mood the moment we stepped into the United States. An "ordinary" Canadian citizen and, especially, a native of Colombia, she has had her experiences with feeling discriminated against because of where she came from, her skin colour, her accent, and so on. Consequently, Bárbara is always surprised at how easy and pleasant an experience it can be for me to cross over to the United States. This time, it became a subject of conversation (in Spanish, naturally).

"I think I now know why you are so happy every time we go across this border. I think it is because you come from here."

Bárbara and I have a close relationship in all aspects. I will here talk briefly about the evolution of our ability to communicate on the intellectual-spiritual level. Even in our first days together, when she was only beginning to understand some French – the language in use on our Reserve – she quickly set out to be my special assistant and even adviser in my work as a Native historian. Her rare perceptiveness soon enabled her to begin helping with the typographical part of my writing (it was only during my sabbatical leave that year that I found time to learn how to type with a set method), and quite quickly also to know when her ideas about what I was writing or doing professionally could be useful, or were necessary.

In that way, someone who had never been exposed to our Native reality or studies and, moreover, was only beginning to learn the French and English languages became almost overnight a critical though invisible adviser to the person soon to become the first Canadian Amerindian to obtain a doctoral degree in history (in 1991). What is also to Bárbara's great credit, those doctoral studies were undertaken in good part because she insisted that my newly earned MA in history was not going to allow me to properly represent and defend my Indian people in my chosen discipline because "most non-Indian historians and other non-Native academics would not allow me to stand on an equal footing with and among them." Even though this meant we were going to have to keep struggling financially, Bárbara made me decide to do four more years of study in order to become my people's first academically certified historian.

Bárbara is a Colombian by birth and is deeply conscious and proud of her Indigenous heritage. Our son is named Miguel after our ancestor Michel Tsioui, a great Wendat Chief of the nineteenth century, and because of Bárbara's loving remembrance of her Indian grandfather on her mother's side. Her father, whom she also revered and who left this world in 1967, was of pure Spanish origin. The philosophy that we share, however, is that being Indian and Indigenous is all about finding how we can help address the problems that our world faces as a global entity and, in unity with other human beings, apply that thinking and that knowledge in humane, constructive ways. Our shared vision is that the social and spiritual crisis that grips the world has reached such huge and menacing proportions that, despite the often extreme colonial duress historically and still presently experienced by most of our Indigenous peoples, no group, society, or nation should think itself morally entitled to set itself apart from the rest of humanity and demand special treatment merely and irresponsibly on the basis of having endured colonial violence.

While they should first be conducive to ensuring the well-being of communities, educational systems in force among any group, society, or nation should also be geared toward engendering a reflection on how a particular group, society, state, or nation can use its own cultural, intellectual, and spiritual heritage to create or help create solutions to problems and dangers faced by other communities or by the whole global human and environmental community.

Individuals such as Bárbara and I view, with worry and sadness, the way in which many individual Indians and many Indigenous communities have been made to lose their sense of their own strength, independence, and importance. Instead, they come to rely, as a means to live and survive, on reminding society of how and how much they have been historically victimized. I, for my part, come from a people extremely diminished in terms of its physical presence and strength amid modern society but that thinks itself unaffected in its traditional role and responsibility to be a leader in relation to all other peoples, and especially to the newcomers who need to be taught how to relate harmoniously to their newly found motherland, their Eatenonha. My parents and my forebears taught me, taught us, that there is absolutely no time to be a victim and, most of all, that acting so would amount to betraying our proud and loving ancestors and disregarding the work they have done over millennia in order to build the beautiful civilizations of which we, the First Peoples, are the first heirs.

Bárbara is a Native of her country and, as I have already hinted at, possesses the same kind of Indigenous pride I have just been describing. She is deeply humane and compassionate and has impeccable respect for all people. However, she cannot harbour the thought, much too current in our societies, that Indigenous peoples are less able than other peoples or must accept to live lives of lesser quality because they are Indigenous. On the contrary, like other traditional Native people, including myself, she thinks that as original *dueños* (masters) of this continent, Indigenous people have the duty to always strive to hold their place as descendants of its First Peoples, thus as builders of the rich civilizations that have contributed to renewing and enriching the world as it is now known. That is how Bárbara and I are of one mind about our history as First Nations of the Americas and about our responsibilities as their heirs.

"I think I know why you are so happy every time we go across this border. I think it is because you come from here," Bárbara said to me that day in February 2012. Our next stop for gas was to be Syracuse, New York, after which we continued down to the state of Maryland and spent our first night on the road in the stylish, cozy, brand-new Country Inn, in Wallaceburg. "It was in these parts that you lived the first seven months of your life inside your mother's womb," Bárbara said. Then added, "I think that you are quite different, in many ways, from everyone else in your family because you come from a different place; you were conceived and lived in this environment."

She said this also knowing very well that my family has a unique history among the rest of the population of our Reserve. Quite early on in our married life, Bárbara peremptorily remarked that the reason my family and some others were not regarded well, not treated fairly on the Reserve, was that we "were not from there," and thus "would never be really accepted." She made that observation once she had been duly informed, especially by my mother, Éléonore, that some Huron families, including both my maternal and my paternal families, had had their own separate community, named the Forty Arpents Reserve. It was there that we, the self-styled "last authentic descendants of the original Huron Nation now living in the Province of Quebec,"[2] lived for two centuries and pertinaciously, even heroically, held on to our land and our identity until we were defeated by both State and Church in 1904. Many of our thirty or so families were forced to settle on the main Reserve of Village-des-Hurons (today renamed Wendake). Some of those families dispersed to different locations, a few ending up going to the United States, and some, like my mother's people, deciding they would do their utmost to stay on their old Reserve, even though it thenceforth became the French-Canadian parish of Saint-Gérard-Magella (now renamed Val-Bélair). Emery Sioui, my mother's father, was, until 1935, the last Chief of the remaining Siouis of the Forty Arpents.

CHAPTER TWO

SEAWI: HURONS OF THE RISING SUN

In order to begin to give to you, dear reader, as clear an idea as I can about the social and political atmosphere in which I was raised, I present my translation of an unpublished text I wrote in French, in 1980, and that bears the title "Seawi:[1] Hurons du Soleil Levant" ("Seawi: Hurons of the Rising Sun"). Much of the information contained in this piece, written in the latter part of my youth, will provide bridges whereby you, my reader, can enter a time nearer than the present one to what I perceive was an Aboriginal, unbroken feeling of my people about their intimate character and their sovereign sense of pride. Such time, I much regret to say, is now forever gone from the Wendat (Huron) reality in our community and it has now become our duty to inscribe it in our national history so that it can become part of the human and Canadian heritage.

Once situated at the very heart of northeastern North America, our Wendat Nation was, because of the Europeans' arrival, one of the most severely depopulated on our continent. Having numbered between 30,000 and 40,000 at the time of contact, our Nation (we were, in fact, a confederacy of five nations) has now been reduced to a few thousand descendants who live on or claim affiliation to two Reserves: one in Canada, close to Quebec City, named Village-des-Hurons (now renamed Wendake) and the other, situated in northeastern Oklahoma, named Wyandotte. Two other communities, one in Canada and the other in the US, are not judicially recognized by these two nation-states; they are the Wyandots of Anderdon, in southeastern Ontario, and the Wyandots of Kansas, mostly centred in Kansas City. Other descendants of the Huron-Wyandot, few in numbers, live dispersed in diverse parts of Canada and the United States. In total, we are some 3,000–4,000 descendants, still fighting proudly and hard against the forces of assimilation and obliteration of our very memory.

I am a Huron, grandson of four Huron grandparents. My family is one of traditionalists and we have good knowledge of our greater Indian family. If I were to characterize my Nation in a few words, I would say that we are quite markedly lucid about the sense of our history, that we have no illusions, and harbour almost no prejudice about anyone. Our history is almost unknown by non-Indians, who only think they know it. It is a long, very sad, and beautiful history. Listening to this brief relation of it will make any person richer and happier.

Made stronger by a tradition of more than 500 years of contact with the original child of the Great Island on the Turtle's Back (as our ancestors named their continent), by healthy air, pure waters, and new-found freedom on this sacred land, the American descendant of the children who once took refuge or immigrated here from the "old countries" has gone through a profound evolution, both in mind and body. On the physical level, he is generally stronger and healthier than his European ancestors; on the mental and spiritual planes, he is more tolerant of differences. His manner of creating governance has become somewhat similar to those that characterize the civilization of the Aboriginal inhabitants: his religions are less dogmatic and oppressive and more universal. His psyche has gotten used to abundance and he has largely freed himself from the antique fears and anguish inherited from long ages he has known civil and religious tyranny. He educates himself to doubt the healthiness of his living habits, stammers about ecology, and opens his eyes on the beauty of the environment, which he still does not see as his Mother Earth.

For the future harmony of our societies, it is extremely important that we plant in our collective subconscious those seeds of understanding of our pasts and of our origins. You and I have been defrauded of the possibility of this understanding and we are still paying an inhumanly high price for having been made orphans of our histories and of our memory. Our knowledge has been extorted from us while our natural desire to communicate it to others has been crushed; our alliances have been mutilated and their memory buried. In that graveyard of our wisdom and of our dreams of liberation were cultivated hatred, false glories, guilt, ignorance, fear, and spiritual emptiness.

My father had often said to me, "One day soon, the Indians (our people) will cease to cry, for Time is the Father of Truth." My mother, who had always had a burning desire to learn and to know (to make that same truth of which my father spoke spring forth) and who also wanted to preserve her children from the sterile, even nefarious experience of Reserve life, succeeded in getting me admitted to the second year of the primary school when I was only five years old (after a brief four months of private schooling to complete the first year).

As I am, by nature, contemplative, I only rarely was fully aware of school and where I found myself. In my mind, I was almost constantly outside, over yonder, amid nature. I only came back momentarily when a comrade would tug at my sleeve to tell me that the nun was asking me a question, to which, with a face suddenly quite reddened and my body broken out in a cold sweat, I only rarely knew what to answer. I was discomfited every time to see and feel that nun's extreme and holy wrath and confused for having recreated that too familiar scenario that regularly caused the whole class to burst out laughing. Blessed by I have never known which saint, the *curé* of our Reserve was something of a philosopher who soon advised the nuns to "leave that boy to think," since I managed to get passable marks, which my mother and father, incomprehensibly enough for my young, already-a-tad-conditioned mind, told me were excellent. It is thus that this dear cleric saved me from the strap, then utilized to punish the "bad" pupils, and from the many shattering consequences that physical blows have on the future of children who often prefer being "in the moon" rather than on the Earth with dumb, unloving people.

A DEFINING MOMENT[2]

Very early in my school career (the following year), I was drawn out of one of my daydreams by the word *savage*, which reached me in the quiet depths of the forests where I was wandering that afternoon. I rushed into combat just like one of my Huron ancestors when threatened, only to find myself confronted by a fat, black-robed nun. She glared at me, her thick dark eyebrows streaks of war paint rising to the starched white helmet beneath her veil. Her pointer tapped as she walked and talked, her words harsh, her tone reproving, conscious of the devastating effect she must make on our young minds. It was her duty to implant a system of values and morality that would wipe out every shred of respect we might still feel for our ancestors and for the dignity of their life. She was a fountain of truths that we must never doubt, under threat of spiritual and very possibly physical death.

"Your poor ancestors were savages," she had said. "They didn't know the Good Lord. When Jacques Cartier and Sieur de Champlain discovered Canada and founded New France, they saw your ancestors worshipping the sun and idols. They saw them kill and eat other savages. Fortunately, the savages were afraid of the Frenchmen's guns. Sieur Cartier and Sieur de Champlain tried to teach them the Faith, but the savages were too ignorant to understand it. The King took pity on them and sent missionaries to convert them, but your savage ancestors killed the missionaries. They became our Holy Canadian Martyrs who died to save the savages."

Moved almost to tears, she made us kneel and pray for forgiveness from the Holy Canadian Martyrs for our ancestors' cruelty, urging them to intercede with God for the conversion of savages in Canada and elsewhere. "With the help of God, the nuns, and priests," she went on, "you have now become civilized people. You should ask God's forgiveness every day for the sins of your ancestors and thank Him for giving you the Catholic faith and snatching you from the hands of Satan, who kept your savage ancestors in a state of idolatry, deceitfulness, thievery, war, and cannibalism. Stand up; we're going to sing a hymn of thanks to the Blessed Virgin." We rose and the good sister began, her voice loud and shrill as she sang one of her favourite hymns, already familiar to some of us. I noticed that almost all my classmates hung their heads. A little girl two desks behind me was sobbing. I, however, had already decided to tell my father about this episode and be guided by him.

Before dismissing class for the day, the nun – we called her "Mother" – proudly announced she was going to start teaching us our national anthem. "You'll know it at the same time as the big boys and girls in the third and fourth grades. I'm teaching it to them this year too. You'll be able to sing along with them on prize day," she added in a cheerful tone that failed to charm us. "You must learn it as a prayer," she persevered, "because it's more of a prayer than a hymn. It expresses not only our pride in being Canadians, but even more our pride in being Christians." She coughed several times to clear her throat, then, at the top of her lungs, proceeded to murder the fine melody of "O Canada" with ear-splitting relish. With the first line, *"terre de nos aïeux"* ("our home and native land"), I at last returned, if only briefly, to my forests and philosophical explorations in the land of my ancestors, conscious of the distant echo of a cawing crow ... *croix, exploits, droits.*

The sound of the hall bell rung by a fourth grader (fourth graders were the oldest pupils in the Reserve school) brought me back to the classroom. It was getting noisy, but not as noisy as on most days, I noticed. The sister completed her day with the comment, "Don't forget confession tomorrow. Begin examining your consciences. You must clean house to be ready for Jesus on Sunday." We all filed past her, slower, more subdued, with heads hanging lower than usual as we intoned our mechanical farewell. "Bonsoir Mère, merci Mère."

Outside, in a dull, cool, already ending day of March, I found myself walking at the side of a girl from our class. She looked at me for an instant and quickly hid again her beautiful black Huron eyes, and I imagined her drowning in a feeling of sorrow as immense as life itself. She began sobbing more intensely. My own heart grew heavier and I too began to weep, perhaps because

I could not help her, perhaps because I thought that she, like I, was grieving over the fate of our dear ancestors, destroyed, then despised, perhaps because I thought that no one in the world could help her, and perhaps also because she was very beautiful. We thus walked until we reached the house where she lived, which was not far, without looking at each other or being able to speak even a word. I continued to the edge of the woods to hear the river, which, like every spring, was recovering the full power of its voice. When I made it home, a little late, I felt strangely consoled: it must have been the grandiose power and beauty of Nature, awaking after the long winter. Nevermore, however, did I walk alongside that friend of an erstwhile sorrow of wounded Huron children, whom my six-year-old eyes found so beautiful. (Like most of our young women, she married young, with a white man.)

FATHERS AND SONS

My father, Georges-Albert, had grown up in proud admiration of his father, reputedly one of the best hunters and certainly the most renowned Indian guide of his time (he lived eight-nine years). In many parts of the land, as well as in the United States, Paul Sioui was known for his dexterity in every manner of woodcraft, his imperturbable tranquility, his wisdom, his subtle and pacifying sense of humour, and his physical strength. His witticism sometimes became the source of enduring debates and new stories known and repeated among the Circles of Forest Philosophers, and some of his exploits in the woods had even appeared in some daily newspapers. My grandfather was a man of few words; people spoke in praise of him, but it was almost impossible to make him speak about himself. Fairly often, with just a few words, "the Chief," as he was called by his fellow woodsmen, brought an end to a discussion that had lasted an hour but was not leading to any clarifying conclusion, thus provoking mirthful laughter among all reasoners present.

Paul Sioui knew that his life had been a success but that those times in the history of our people were inexorably coming to an end: the time of the great hunts when Indians, in spite of all the

contempt that society showed for them, still had a material role
to play in the protection of their motherland – upon whom they
found rest, joy, counsel, and solace – and saw time spent away
from her as time wasted. Those times when our Huron ancestors met in the woods in all intimacy and warmth their Abenaki,
Montagnais, Maliseet, Algonquin, Attikamek, Mi'kmaq, Cree, and
also Canadian[3] brothers, helping one another, hunting, fishing,
guiding, laughing, smoking, playing, sleeping together in their tents
or in their *cabanes* upon their Mother Earth's belly. Carefree about
banks, bosses, professors, history books, or about tomorrow, times
which many laypeople today simplistically like to say were hard.
However, the more initiated folks think and still talk about those
times as having been hard within human proportions, times when
most humans knew that in the larger scheme of life joys are necessarily greater than sorrows since life always wins out: Can there
exist greater misery than having the freedom to rest in the sun only
a few weeks in the year? Is there poverty more extreme than not
being able to look after one's old parents and thus denying one's
children access to those treasures of knowledge and education in
the sacred sense of the Circle of Life?

My father's father and his contemporaries knew well that
time was expiring. The subconscious mind of the Indian and of
perhaps even more of the Huron, for reasons that are obvious
enough and that we have set about to elucidate, is steeped in the
stark reality of (his post-contact) history. During the thirty years
that I knew this grandfather (he left us in 1978), never could I
or my brothers get him to speak the way we would have wished
about the woods, the Indian life, his travels, his memories. It was
only a few months before he left "for the other country" that
he confided in me about a dream that he had long had of *un
beau campe*[4] on the shore of his favourite river, thus giving a
very rare glimpse of all his hopes of justice and happiness. To
all our questions, subtle or direct, asked when we had a chance
to see him during his brief appearances in the village, he would
only have this answer, "Take your pencils, study and learn." He
usually illustrated that sentence with a movement of his hand as
if it were handling a pencil and would say something witty but

frankly disconcerting to us, such as: "Soyez les premiers de la tête, pas les premiers de la queue." (Be the first from the head down, not the first from the tail down.) We would understand only later. We, his grandsons, have long doubted his good sense and often thought that he did not love us, and he knew that too. When his final hour was approaching, in his home, in his bed, his whole being radiated perfect serenity. I told him how well I knew that he had been loving and wise toward us, his grandchildren. I also said to him that when one day I would have a son, he would carry his name. He nodded weakly. One last time, I looked at his face and I saw the goodness, the nobleness, and the moral strength of the old Hurons. Our two souls joined forever in the infinity of our glance. I told him: "Merci, grand-papa," and went. He left us the day after.

My father had heard much of the story of the expulsion of his father and the whole Huron community from the former Forty Arpents Reserve without any compensation for the loss of everything they possessed, not even, as my maternal grandmother often related to us, the paltry six dollars per head promised by the government. My grandfather had also lived through the theft of his people's hunting territories and timberlands by the colonial governments whose agents had promised to "take the savages out of those parts" if they got elected. Some of their relatives and tribal members had also met their mysterious end in the forest because, as it is still believed among us, they had dared return to their former hunting grounds. My father had seen his father, his uncles, and those who did not want to become broken men on social assistance begin a life as illegal hunters and seasonal guides for wealthy American and other tourists on the lands that had been ripped away from their Native children and rented to these *messieurs* for a hundred years.

Paul Sioui also observed the original Hurons becoming a minority on their Reserve, losing any meaningful political weight through a conspiration of the Church and the governments who jointly manoeuvred the adoption of several "Canadian" families and granted them legal Indian status. This helped make our Reserve a model Reserve, thereby enabling the federal government to justify the application in other Native communities across the country of the most overtly racist program of assimilation of the First Peoples. Even worse for us, these tactics would make it more difficult to achieve the unity that was so necessary to our Nations in the Province of Quebec and, consequently, in the whole country itself. It is for all of this that my grandfather told us, his grandchildren, to get a formal education and to grasp our pens and learn how to write. It is for all these reasons that he had wished to make of my father a "man of the pen."

Georges-Albert Sioui was naturally gifted. I was often told that the young man who was to be my father shone in everything he applied his mind to. In primary school, without exerting too much effort, Georges-Albert's marks were very good and he soon tired of that captive existence, dedicating his attention instead to the manlier exercises of sports and life in the woods. It is opportune to remark here that many Indians of that generation, the immediate heirs of the "last true Indians of the forest," possessed and demonstrated outstanding talents and aptitudes that regrettably very few had a chance to cultivate enough to make a contribution to the outside world.

At that time, the better my father did out of school, the more he neglected his classes and the lower were his marks. When he returned from his long hunting seasons, his father, far from applauding to the athletic prowess of his eldest son, showed strong disappointment at his apparent lack of interest in his education. "Do you think you will succeed in life just playing and dreaming, my son? Do you not understand that the time when we could make a living with the forest is now over and gone?" Then came down the verdict from a father too often and for too long obliged to hunt and toil alone, away from his loved ones: "I will go and meet with the Head Friar of the college and tell him to use all means possible to get you to study as you should." The religious staff, in those days often ill-meaning racists, made a feast of the situation. They so frequently beat my father that my poor heartbroken grandmother had to take her sixteen-year-old son out of that institution. She tried her best to make her husband understand that such educational experience could well ruin the life of their son and that perhaps the forest could be what would make of him the man he dreamed of becoming.

Early in the spring of his seventeenth year, my father left for the woods on an expedition due to last two months during which he, his father, and four other true Huron woodsmen were to build a log camp and get everything ready – the territory, the portages, the canoes, the docks, and a hundred other things – for the arrival in a few months' time of the "gentlemen" (wealthy members of the Hunting and Fishing Club). Three thousand pounds of provisions and building materials to carry through trails, lakes, and rivers over a distance of thirty miles (this was before the conversion to the metric measures in Canada). Never once did my grandfather lend a hand or give advice to his greenhorn of a son, while the other four men had to risk doing so behind the Chief's back. My father told me how hard he had to strain to keep up with the pace of these "ironmen" who only rarely stopped to smoke their pipe or a *pollock* (a hand-rolled cigarette) and make tea and who could carry a cast-iron stove over hour-long portages on what were often no more than moose trails in swampy, rocky terrain. My father still recounts how happy and proud he felt when they all got installed in their small camp. A place where all became still, even the wind, for the nightly concert of the frogs, the loons, and the owls; in that very vast domain where no one nor a thing in the world could impede them in feeling they were the lords and original children. He was proud and happy to be able to live alongside these five masters of every woodcraft and in whose hearts and minds he believed was stored all the world's wisdom. He was able to piously listen to their hours of silence and their illuminating words, far away from all vain competitions and contentions, in a school where the animals were teachers, where time and the spirits of earth and sky dictated every rule.

My father came back to our village after almost a year – half a foot taller, a man, strong and mature – knowing himself worthier of the father he venerated who had become proud of this first son. Above all, Georges-Albert came back imbued for life with a deepened, sovereign pride of being an Indian and a Huron: a descendant of the Wendat, the heart-people of the Northeast of our America, our Great Island, which at the beginning of time, our Grandfather the Big Turtle ordered to be established on his back.

To be sure, my father had become a ripe young man; however, at that time when an economic crisis was affecting the whole world, it was not possible for a young person to think of founding a family on the meagre seasonal wages of a hunting and fishing guide, not even with the supplement coming from the trapping of fur animals. At twenty-one years old, my father met the woman of his life, my mother, a Huron and first child of one of the few families to have remained in the former Forty Arpents after the dispersal of 1904. My maternal grandfather, Emery Sioui, was a renowned hunter and the founder of a world-class fur animal ranch. He was also the last Chief of the traditionalist off-Reserve Hurons. My parents' respective families, remotely related, had always known each other but belonged, after the dispersal, to two very distinct worlds – the Reserve and the vast outside world.

When the Second World War broke out, my father had to flee (after physically defeating two military officers sent to our Reserve to force our young men to enrol) to the United States to avoid the conscription that was imposed on Indian nations despite the laws in vigour at the time. This principle of non-involvement in the "white man's wars" was rigorously observed by the great majority of Hurons, even more so because our Nation was fortunate to have access to more socio-economic outlets than the majority of Indian nations. Oftentimes, many of these populations saw important numbers of their youth enrol in the military to escape from the hunger and misery that, then and now, plague many Reserves. Very pointedly also, our Native communities acted with the purpose of achieving standards of living that would reflect the dignity of our peoples, their contributions, and the sacrifices they would and did endure to make possible the existence of this wonderful country named Canada, revered by all her inhabitants and envied by the whole world. They were frequently encouraged in this endeavour by the governments only to be bitterly deceived because of the inaction and the systemic racism characteristic of these governing entities.

At the end of the war, my father came back to the land of his love to get married. Once more, he turned to the forest to make a living for his little family (my sister Carole was born eleven months after his return), but soon realized that his father had been right: "Let us look toward the future," the Chief was wont to say. The newlyweds thus left for the United States with their "beautiful red-haired doll," as my father called his adored daughter, where a millionaire client of my grandfather's hired my father in one of this jewel factories. However, my parents had already decided that my mother would come back to Canada so that the one writing these lines would not be born in the United States and perchance become defender of a foreign ideology, inimical to the Earth, instead of protector of this same Earth, mother of us all.

Like a great number of young Native men faced with the fact that they henceforth would have to earn a living within a system in which they neither could have faith nor feel a true emotional attachment, my father began to resort to alcohol, bottled illusions of strength and freedom. Living became impossible without that "remedy," broken as he was in his Indian way of understanding life. Nevermore was he going to feel real, simple happiness now forever separated from nurturing Mother Earth, wise counsellor of all his ancestors before him. Still today, grown old before his time because of his dire addiction, my father only lives for the rare occasions that we, his sons, find the time to take him with us to our ancestral forests; an offence to the laws that very few of our people dare commit because of the severity of the legal consequences for those who contravene.[5] Then, and only then, my father no longer has thirst for his poor, wretched remedy that keeps him sick while killing his pain. And my father is only one Indian.

A NEW PATH

During the weekend that followed this rough initiation to Canada's history, I was not able to speak to my father. He was probably out drinking with some friends. I would have asked my mother the questions that were on my mind, but I felt that, alone and poor, with five children already at the time, she was much too overwhelmed for me to even think of speaking to her about the insults that the sister had splashed on our people that Friday afternoon. We were already sufficiently burdened with the social consequences of those insults and those lies. My mother had first to find enough food for us. Maybe some of her patients would call her to come down to Quebec City (fifteen kilometres from our Reserve) and heal them with her excellent natural remedies, and maybe she would be successful in selling a few pairs of Indian moccasins (supple footwear ever in demand). She would then come back by evening time, her arms full of the cheapest but healthiest (and for us, her "little ones" waiting for her in the familial nest, the best) food that she could find, with perhaps a little surprise for the older kids who were more apt to appreciate the efforts of our heroine, which my mother was for us. After a good meal, she would sing us a lullaby, taking us on her lap two by two or three by three before putting us to bed after saying a prayer that she always created according to life as we lived it. Finally, she would go to sleep, worn out and too often alone.

My questions had become more precise in my head when at last, later in the week, my father arrived early with a little money for mother. After they had quarrelled, forgiven each other, and reconciled, the time came for our so long-awaited wrestling session. We were five children then:[6] Carole, our eldest; me; Vincent, who showed real talent for wrestling; the tiny but tough Régent; and Konrad, our baby, standing and tottering in his crib, totally absorbed in our bouts. Papa was good at feigning that we were giving him a real hard time and would always end up bursting into laughter at seeing how much heart we were putting in the game, certainly reminiscing about his own character as a young boy. I was always astonished at Vincent's efficiency in coordinating our assaults and making every little shred of our forces count. Carole, like in everything she did, gave our dad special pride. Régent, by instinct, attacked the neck and glanced at us as if saying, "All-out attack! Look at the hold I got on him!" We looked at one another as little as possible for fear of losing strength, which, at any rate, always had the happy effect of making our father laugh until he got totally weak, allowing us to win the round.

But there was always me with my important questions. My father knew it and I often got the impression that he read those in my eyes. Between two wrestling bouts, I told him that I had questions for later. "Of course, my son, something caused you pain at school, I know. We'll talk about that later, after the younger ones have gone to bed." Carole came to cut this short: "Hey, this isn't the time to talk about school. Let's wrestle! OK! We start again!"

This time, Carole and Vincent had made up a plan for a surprise attack. They flung themselves on Papa with lighting speed. Régent took back the neck, and I, both our giant's legs. It was Mother who came to pull her husband away from sure, bitter defeat. "Régent, time for a bath," she said, trying to lift Konrad – our baby with bright red hair – who, standing in his crib, did not miss any of the action and screamed and shouted his applause.[7] Neither he was willing to leave his crib nor Régent his hold on father's neck. In the end they were taken away, still kicking and screaming "like devils in holy water" when Mother lay them in the tub to wash them. As to us, the oldest, Papa inevitably had to lift us up many times at the end of one arm, until Maman shouted to Vincent to get ready for bed, the old bed that he and I shared for many years.

After making us drink some water, Papa sat Carole and me down on his knees. "So, how is it at school?" he asked. "Maman and I are glad about your marks, that is very good; school is very important, you know." "Once again, I got first rank," interjected Carole. "I am very proud of that, my girl, and Georges also is doing very well. As long as one does one's best, that's what counts." (My father was thus giving a subtle excuse for the fact that my schooling achievements were still rather ordinary because, as my parents rightly thought, of my very early start in school.) "The mother, in class, said that our ancestors were savages," I hastened to say with, I believe, some emotion in my voice. "She said that our ancestors killed the priests and everyone else and we prayed to ask for God's forgiveness." "It's not even true, is it, Papa?" Carole carried on. "She made Anne weep, the daughter of your great friend Roland," I added, stopping at this point. Straightening his back, my father looked in my eyes in the serious but soft way you do when speaking to someone who has been hurt. He said to me, "In your life, my son, you will often hear people talk ill about our people. When the French people and other Europeans arrived here in our land, we the Indians were, as we still are, peaceful and generous people. Often, the Europeans were sick, and we cared for them. Many times, our ancestors fed them with good food. As is our way, we have treated them as relatives, and we have taught them how to live well, here in our homeland.

"Many Europeans became jealous because we had such a beautiful and good country and because we lived in peace with nearly all the other Indian peoples. To rob us of our country, they invented the pretext that we had no religion. They sent religious missionaries among the Hurons; those priests and the other Frenchmen unwittingly propagated very powerful diseases that made many of our people die. When the French priests wrote the history of Canada, they lied when they related that the Indians had almost all killed one another. Our ancestors were true Christians because they assisted one another and were too busy observing and protecting Nature to make war between themselves. The Europeans spent a lot of time warring and robbing from one another instead of helping one another. It is for those reasons that many of them were sick and so much envied our beautiful country, as their own countries were ruined.

"It is God who allows everything to be, my son. It is He who governs us, and He is never mistaken. It is He who has willed the white people to come here so that we could help them learn how He wants us, humans, to live. A day will come when they will realize the harm that they do to themselves by not respecting God's creation. That day, they will ask God to forgive and to save them. That day, the Indian people will begin to play an important part for peace to exist in the world, for many people of many nations will tell us that they wish to know us and to listen to us. Most people are good, my son, and have a sense of what truth is. One day, all people together will re-establish the government of God, the Great Spirit, the One that our people know and accept.

"Never believe the ones who will tell us that our people are not good and that theirs is the best one. There are good and bad people in every nation. Canada's history is deceitful. You are the ones who will have to correct it, when you are older. The people who come to live in our country need to know the truth, they don't enjoy being left in ignorance. For now, do not argue with the ones who teach you. In your classwork, write what you need to write in order to obtain good marks. When, one day, you are in the higher grades and in university, you will get the opportunity to look for the true facts and to write them down. That is what you will need to do, as Huron Indians. Always remain polite and kind to everyone; people will treat you the same way." "I got 95 per cent in History, Papa," said Carole, after a moment. "That is excellent, my girl, Papa has seen it in your class report," proudly answered our father, who had now leaned back in his armchair. As to myself, I not only felt relieved but also happy to be given a sense of my life's duty, already traced by my father himself. I felt enormous pride for having this father. Never was I to speak a word to anyone about this pact he and I had just sealed together. "Papa, Mother Superior wants to teach us the song of 'O Canada!' It says that Canada is the land of their ancestors. I don't want to sing that." "Then you just do not sing it," said my father, straightening his back once again. "Besides, I will go to see Sister Saint-Jean-de-Brébeuf tomorrow morning. Papa will surely help her understand, she is a good person. People often don't know any better, we must be kind to her too."

"I am tired," said Carole, stretching arms and neck to hug Papa. "All right children, we will speak again tomorrow, it is getting late. Go and kiss Maman good night," ended my father, stooping to hug both Carole and me. We went to the living room where Maman was still sewing. "You look happy, my dear boy," she said to me with her own radiant smile. "You are going to write books, later on, aren't you? That will be marvellous. Good night, my boy. You will help me to write also." Her strong, joyous embrace made me say that I would, in a tone meant to hide my enthusiasm, for I hadn't imagined that she knew. There would only be the four of us. "Carole also will teach many beautiful and important things." Hugging Maman, she too said, "Yes." We said good night to her and went up to our rooms. "Do not forget to pray, you now are able to do it on your own. Tomorrow, we will pray together."

Before going to bed, I went to Carole's room where we had, in hushed voices, our first theological exchange. "Carole," I began, "I never know what to say when I am at confession. I never have anything to say." "You have to listen when the sister reads the list of sins," answered Carole, using a severe tone that also intimated that my marks could also improve if I listened better in class. "I do listen," I replied, "but I always have the thought that it is impossible to sin because it is impossible that one wills to offend God on purpose." "If you think in this way, there is a real danger that you could go to hell," she retorted, less with words than with her beautiful brown eyes that commanded so much respect in me and in the schoolyard where she reigned as defender of our family against our enemies (whose motives for being our enemies I had, in my reproachable ingenuousness, already given up on understanding). "Hell doesn't even exist," was my resolute reply. "In any case, I have never committed a sin, and neither will I ever do so. As Papa has said, 'as long as one does one's best.' There is no such thing as hell, it is only for scaring us." "The sister has said that everyone, even the greatest saints, commits at least seven sins every day," retorted Carole, a bit shaken. "The sister must have told this to your class" (Carole was in third grade in the *classe des grands*). "It's not true," I answered animatedly – thinking at that moment of our grandmother Caroline Dumont, our mother's mother, the curer. "Grand-maman never commits a sin." "You will not get to Heaven," concluded my saddened sister Carole. "I do not want to go to that Heaven, it is much too boring," I darted to my big sister, imagining I was appearing to her as one of those devils whose images the nuns were wont to show us in class. The mere thought of that place of draperies, cotton wool, and flannel blankets where, to the sound of golden trumpets, people were to be and remain forever, adoring God – a bearded old man seated on a rich throne – quite frankly made me feel sick.

I just had to say to my sister, "I will go to the Indians' Heaven. There, we are going to have a good time." Carole went toward the door and said, "We must sleep now. Go say your prayer, it will perhaps help you think better." "In any case, never believe all those lies," I insisted in conclusion, speaking through my sister's closed door, that so dear sister who was my unassailable rampart when the big boys, much older but almost all shorter and weaker than me, cornered and forced me to wrestle against a lad of their "band"; I, who ignored almost everything about the underhanded games that make the pleasure of so many and who never felt the slightest need of defending myself or, much less still, of striking someone else. "Then you can defend yourself alone," came the apprehended, though meaningless answer.

The following morning, my father, very elegant in his policeman's uniform (and besides, a handsome man), walked us to school holding our hands. Carole and I shall never forget how very proud we felt and how we wished to take our time so as to be well seen and looked at by all.[8] When we arrived at the main entrance of the school, where the "mother of the smaller ones" (*la mère des petits*) was always posted to receive the pupils and take note of the late arrivals, my father asked to see Mother Superior. "Certainly, sir," answered the young nun, ostensibly impressed by this police officer, tall and of strong and agreeable appearance. My father wished us a good day and then went up the stairs, following the nun who was my regular teacher. With all the other kids come to see and observe our father, we went down to the play hall to wait for the bell, which soon rang out.

That afternoon, Mother Superior made her entry into our classroom to give us the history lesson. She asked our teacher to say the prayer and to stay for this class. This time, I knew I had to pay close attention. I have kept faithfully enough the essence of the lecture she gave.

She began: "You know, in times before, we used to call your ancestors 'the savages.' It wasn't peoples' fault; they didn't go to school and didn't know the proper words. Nowadays, we say Indians. Your people are as acceptable as the white people, you are Christians just like we are, sometimes even better Christians than the white people. If someone calls you savage, tell them that one cannot use that word because it means that someone is not able to behave as a human being should. There are such people in all races. You must be proud of your ancestors, they have oftentimes given help to the settlers when the colony first started, but the settlers have not always understood your ancestors. They have taken away the lands from the Indians and they have forced them to live in small Reserves, like this one, your Reserve of Notre-Dame-de-la-Jeune Lorette.[9] The Indians have forgiven them, but we must pray so that one day all humans can understand better how to live with one another. When I teach you about Canadian history, don't be afraid to ask me questions and to express your ideas. And when we read from the books, we will always replace the word *savage* with the word *Indian*."

At last, I had found enough open-mindedness and empathy to begin taking an interest in my life as a schoolboy. I had found a purpose, a reason, as well as respect for our people. It seems to me, today, that at the same time as in my own soul, a minute star had just begun to shine in the long night of a people that was losing the very memory of daylight. My marks made a jump and I felt myself more and more mindful of reality as it occurred, for I had found myself a dream that I could live.

Thus began, very slowly and mutedly, an ever-deeper questioning about the pedagogical principles in force in the Indian schools of the Province of Quebec. Following my own example, some of the pupils in our class began refusing to sing the Canadian national anthem and that old practice, still yesterday so firmly rooted, began falling by the wayside into desuetude. Three years later, when most of these school comrades and I found ourselves attending the white school just outside the Reserve, my father, with the support of our Nation's Council and of many of our citizens, obtained from that school's authorities that the Huron children be exempted from standing and singing "O Canada." I do not think myself in error in saying that our Huron Nation, one of the most severely reduced in the whole continent, is the only one to have taken that essential step in education. It was a meritorious deed, mostly in Quebec and in Canada, at the beginning of the 1950s when racial prejudice against Indians was a fact of culture as firmly established and familiar as the promontory of Cap-aux-Diamants in nearby Quebec City.

As for myself, and I know that most of my childhood comrades have done likewise, I have dutifully observed that custom,[10] born from a Huron fact of culture. I know that when that notion of universal human respectability has been imparted to the majority of Indians and our Canadian relatives, we will jointly compose together a national anthem that we will all salute in sincerity and in true unity, at long last.

To be Indian means, before all, to take up the challenge of the truth, without which there is no respect, no desire to share, no communion of hearts. That is what our Indian forebears have fought for, not to destroy one another and amass riches using the apparently most reasonable excuses, but out of their human duty to defend their truth that they knew was inscribed within their hearts. They had never been "warriors" before seeing attacked their right, and that of Nature itself, to exist and be free.

By taking up in their turn and in their own way that challenge of truth, my father, my mother, and their Huron forebears have inspired in their descendants an ability to think and act critically in the defence of our right to be.

It would have been so much easier and socially well seen to let their children's minds be spoiled by false and dishonest notions about their own people without anyone, not even those children themselves, noticing the difference – anyone except, of course, the Indians and the other peoples conventionally seen and treated as negligible. My father could have become an officer of high rank in the police hierarchy, or a rich businessman (he had a remarkable business acumen); perhaps an alcoholic, but socially accepted, like so many people. My mother could have afforded courses, jewellery, and expensive trips. We, their children, would probably have become wealthy, mindless individuals, common exploiters and destroyers of the living forces of the poor and of the Earth but unable to see anything abnormal about it. We could also have profited from our "Indian rights" without having to bear the pain that comes with the condition of being Indian. No: out of respect for the fight of their ancestors, my parents have not cheated. They have made warriors of their children, Hurons of the Rising Sun.

CHAPTER THREE

THE SEAWI OF THE FORTY ARPENTS

I belong to the very last family that claims strong roots in the old Forty Arpents Reserve.[1] I did not know my grandfather, Chief Emery Sioui, who died ten years before I was born. However, I was the first grandson of my grandmother Caroline Dumont, and her home was and will remain the home where my heart and my spirit were formed. She was a renowned healer and from her I learned how and why everything one does in life, even the writing of history, has to be approached with a compassionate heart, like the process of creating a remedy for the ills of the world, which every one of us suffers from and which are all related to feelings of separation, rejection, loneliness, powerlessness. "All of us, poor humans, live for the same thing: to be happy. And to be happy, we have to make others happy," was her simple philosophy.

My grandmother's parents, Raphaël Dumont and Éléonore Gros-Louis, were skilled Huron artisans who did not hesitate to move to the United States for a few seasons to escape the scarcity of the Reserve, to expose their seven children to the larger world, and to have them learn English. Of course, as Indians, they faced the usual discrimination in many of its forms, but they knew how to grow stronger, and not weaker, from those challenges. Thus, my grandmother became world-savvy, an excellent speaker of English, and eventually, a forewoman for an important glove manufacturing company in Toronto. She could have accepted a marriage proposition from a well-to-do pilot but decided to go back to Village-des-Hurons to tend to

her ailing mother, Éléonore, who soon after died in the arms of
that very loving daughter. Caroline had set her mind and heart
on Emery Sioui, a much-admired man from those combative,
strategic Huron of the Forty Arpents.

I knew the happiest times of my youth on my grandmother's
farm and in the enchanted atmosphere of her home, which was
my real home. Even though we, as a family, had our own house
in Village-des-Hurons, about five miles from my grannie's home
in Saint-Gérard (as "off-Reserve Indians" did not have access to
free education and medical services), I would swiftly and gleefully
run that distance, non-stop, to go and spend a weekend or even an
afternoon *chez grand-maman*. There, far from the small, reduced,
restless, gossipy life of the Reserve, I found my familiar ambience
of abundance, peace, and plenitude: the farm animals – the hens,
ducks, cows, pigs, horses, and my favourite cats and dogs; those of
the forest – the foxes, raccoons, skunks, and the occasional bear;
the crows, robins, blue jays, red cardinals, goldfinches; and all the
equally marvellous and beloved other birds and animals of all
natures and sizes. And then there were so many people, all so different, who came to see grand-maman, the old Indian woman who,
I knew, had so central a place in the lives and in the hearts of so
many people. This was my first school: learning from her how and
why to listen to people and then, how to help and cure them with
a cup of tea (*un bon thé*), oftentimes a hearty country meal, and a
song that she sang and played on her piano with her old, arthritic
doigts-marteaux (fingers in the shape of little hammers). There was
also almost always a remedy made of herbs, roots, barks, or flowers, to whom she would always have spoken, asking and thanking
them for healing this or that person. Most of all, she would never
forget to acknowledge God, our Creator, and the Good Mother of
Jesus, who is the way to obtain the healing and solicitude for us,
poor humans (*pauvres nous autres*).

My grandmother's world was not only for Indians, quite different from what I sensed life on the Reserve was about. There, it
seemed to me, everyone was competing for being "more Indian"
than everybody else, beginning with the Chief, with his feathers
and almost always his grave, important "white men" around him,

such as the government Indian agent and to be sure, the priest, our "missionary." These three men were the triumvirate that my parents (especially my mother) contended with for a long period of her life until she obtained a PhD at sixty-eight years of age and became an authority in her own right, nationwide and worldwide.

My childhood *chez grand-maman* was rich, intense, and happy. There was a world of space, in the fields and in the forest, where we had a hidden pond that was created from a clear, cold brook by my uncle Louis-Philippe (my grandparents' only surviving son, who was like a second father to me). Our two families counted seventeen children (they had ten and we, seven), and together we were a "tribe." At the time, we were unaware that our two families were, in reality, the last remnant of the Huron's historic presence in or close to what had once been (until 1904) the last shred of their erstwhile homeland. Thanks to a great Huron couple, my maternal grandparents, we were able to live a good, indeed beautiful, life there in that land where my whole being has its very strong roots. We were the last free Huron! And I, for one, belong to nowhere else!

The following poem means to tell my reader more about my family's and my own history and identity.[2]

THAT IS ME, THAT IS US

I was born on my Reserve,
a powerful red-headed boy
of thirteen and a half pounds
as fair as fair can be,
counted from day one,
however,
as a future bad Huron
because born of not just one,
but two of the Siouis
that came from the old Reserve stolen
from their people
a mere forty years before
by the respectable, respected and respectful

Reserve authorities, the Triumvirate of
Priest, Indian Affairs Agent and Government-appointed
"Chief."
"Fanatics, still Savages,"
folks had been taught to call us,
Siouis of the Forty-Arpents Reserve,
"bad Indians,"
even though intermarried
four consecutive generations
with French, Irish, Métis women
(which in part explains my particular complexion).

I owe my essential spiritual education
to my maternal grandmother
Caroline Dumont-Gros-Louis,
a proud "cousin," she used to say,
of Gabriel, out there in Manitoba,
the Great Métis strategist.
My grand-mother was
a superb spirit-warrior,
a sage, medicine-person and midwife
who attended to the birth, the life and the death
of nearly all the "Canadiens"
who came to own our Forty-Arpents Reserve
after the theft by Church and State.
All the white folks in Saint-Gérard
worshipped Madame Sioui, the curer,
as well as the memory
of Emery, my grand-father,
the last Chief of our scattered people
who, countless times,
helped, fed and saved them,
the new people who now had our lands.
The Department terminated his Chieftainship in '35.
The great hunter, fur-rancher and Chief died
exhausted from the fight
in '38, at 48.

I have lived on my Reserve,
like good Indians ought to do,
I have felt the rejection of my own
by the new,
card-carrying Indians
and their phoney leaders
well backed up by
Church and State.
In a face white as a speckled trout's belly,
these blue eyes
through which a Savage gazes,
so masterfully concealed,
have seen and felt,
this "savage heart" (a Cree brother has named me so)
has heard through my keen ears,
has smelled through my freckled nose
the killing scorn
felt by all my people.
I am the invisible Indian
who sees and takes notes
of what is done to us
and to our beloved land.
Nothing escapes me.

Yes, there was a high price to pay
(much higher still if they were Siouis)
for the foolish
proud Hurons
who married one of their own:
poverty, discrimination, alcohol, violence;
but there also was
a special kind of pride because
you felt so much at home
in your land,
you were so grateful
that your love for her
made you feel compassion

for all the rootless ones,
made you feel responsible
for teaching, for showing them.
Your love, somehow,
kept you in balance
(Thank you Great Spirit!
Thank you Mother Earth!
Thank you, all our Relations!
Thanks, Grandma!)

I have lived off my Reserve
like all Indians have to do,
who do not like the stale crumbs
thrown at them
and to still have to say "Thanks,"
or spend most days half-dazed
from drink and dope,
or spend a life hitting
the institutional brick walls
with bare fists
and die early
of a heart burned by rage.
I have lived off my Reserve
where an Indian has to stay Indian
though surrounded by un-truth,
assailed by un-beauty
and has to spend half the time
thinking of how to reassure
his white brothers and sisters
that he means no harm,
that it's all a myth,
that we are people
and that it's okay
to laugh at us anyway,
that in fact, we like it,
and half the time trying
to secretly hang on to his pride

while treading the thin ice of prejudice,
many falling through,
many knowing narrow escapes
from the icy, deadly waters
below.
I have left my beloved forest,
my cherished trees I often hug
when we are alone,
my revered animal-relatives
who stay with me in my dreams.
I have written some books
I have gotten a Ph.D.,
made many concessions
to White society (non-essential ones)
because I really wanted to help
all of us to get along.
I have engineered
and won, with my four brothers
in the Supreme Court of our country,
the Sioui Case.
I have been a College dean and a president,
I have dressed expensively,
accumulated many expensive ties
to carry my people highly,
always trying to keep a clean,
savage heart,
alcohol-free since thirty-nine years,
always ready to give a talk,
to give a class,
to give things, money, whatever,
never leaving the battlefield,
perhaps three days a year spent in the bush,
my own Indian Heaven
where I once so intensely lived,
where we so much laughed and worked
and played and prayed
with our Elders

for our children, for our students,
for our people, for all people.
my grand-mother, my Elders,
my father and mother,
my people,
They live forever in my heart.

I have lived in my parents' home,
Mom, Dad and seven of us children
carrying together
the weight of our truth,
training our legs, our backs,
our minds, our spirits,
never complaining
nor pausing to acknowledge
our own valour,
always facing the scorn
without and within our fence
called our Reserve.
I have lived in my parents' home
where my very first steps were taken
to protect my mother
from my dad
(who I so much adored),
when alcohol advised him to beat her.
I tried, I cried so hard
to defend her,
mother, mother earth,
father, father hurt.
I fled my parents' home
as often as I could
and ran all five miles non-stop
to Grandma's place,
to my dogs, cats, hens, cows, pigs,
bears, skunks, squirrels, foxes,
hares, crows and partridges,
to my pond, my forest, my secret places,

to the smell of the birch bark grandma always kept
to light up the old stove
very early on autumn and winter mornings,
and the so dear,
seemingly-gone-for-ever aroma
of the tea of red spruce bark
ever-present on the back-burner,
in the fall and winter;
to the smell of simple country food
spreading with the heat
as the old house thawed out,
every morning,
creaking cheerfully,
my own canary answering merrily
to my skillful canary trills,
both of us wanting to play;
to the last remaining home
in our own Sioui Huronia,
our former Forty-Arpents Reserve
now stolen from us but
where no one denied
our roots so deep, so true,
where all the newcomers
came to see my granny
for a clue, a cheer,
a song on her piano,
a medicine for body and soul,
and went away with a smile,
a new outlook on their
daily struggle for life.
Silently, intently listening
to all that life going on:
such was my real schooling.
One of the proudest moments of my life:
an old Canadien ("White man"),
worrying sincerely about us,
asked the old Indian woman

about her first grandson,
so white-skinned, so red-haired, so blue-eyed:
"Madame Sioui:
how are you going to make an Indian
out of this boy!?!"
My granny took a very serious air
and said to the man, and to the world:
"My grandson here is an Indian through and through!"

That is me. That is us.

THE SEAWI-ONONDAGA CONNECTION

There is a second reason why Bárbara, on that morning of
12 February 2012, when we crossed the United States border,
reflected that my family, my people, had different roots than most
of the folks of the Reserve. Through some odd, almost mysterious
coincidence, our name, *Sioui*, in one of its ancient forms, *Seawi*,
has a very direct historical connection with a hereditary name
in the original Onondaga roster of Civil, or Hereditary Chiefs.
Each of the five original Hodenosaunee (Iroquois) Nations
had a fixed number of such Chiefs, for a total of fifty for the
whole Confederacy. The Onondaga had fourteen Civil Chiefs (or
Royaner, roughly translated to Guardians of the Law of Peace).
Around the 1880s, the number of Civil Chiefs for the whole
Confederacy, or League, became forty-nine and the name that
was withdrawn was Seawi.

The Onondaga traditionalists, apparently, have no certainty
as to how and when the name Seawi came to exist on the roll
call of their *Royaners*. The most reliable documentation,[3] based
on their oral history (perhaps in the mid-1650s), suggests that
at some point in the not-so-ancient history of the Onondaga
Nation, they had "offspring." If we look at the great upheaval
that came with the Europeans' arrival and the heavy population
losses brought about by the resulting wars and epidemics, the
expression of getting "offspring" can quite logically mean that
the Onondaga, like many nations at the time, took in important

numbers of adoptees meant to replenish their ever-endangered numbers. These adoptees were thus designated as "offspring" in the traditional, matrilineal way of thinking, speaking, and structuring societies.

Now, as Bárbara and as everyone knows, my people and I are Wendat and, as is also well known, the Onondaga and the four other Iroquois Nations were at once our close kin and our traditional enemies. Going to less well-known facts, our alliance with the French has meant our eventual, rapid demise. In pre-European times, we, the Wendat, were the most central as well as the most affluent and prosperous of all the nations of northeastern North America, which explains why the French quickly grafted themselves onto us and our vast commonwealth of Native nations. However, the geopolitically and numerically marginal Hodenosaunee (Iroquois), through their alliance with the more commercially astute and free-spirited Dutch who provided them with ample material support, mostly weapons and metal trade goods, soon found themselves in a position of military superiority. Through the massive adoptions that they were thus able to effect, the Hodenosaunee also acquired the wealth of traditional knowledge and the strategic political and commercial connections that they had lacked prior to the Europeans' arrival.

What are of more interest to a woman – to Bárbara in this case – than all this history of wars, conflicts, and power are questions that can help explain the more subtle, or more spiritual meaning of the relationship of the ones she is in society with, such as her life-companion. That day, Bárbara drew my attention to the fact that Syracuse, the place where I was conceived, lies in the heart of Onondaga country. To her, a Colombian-born "new Canadian" with limited knowledge about the Hodenosaunee, the Onondaga, even the Wendat and the relations we had with one another, there is certainly something at play in this connection. There is possibly a key to better understanding who this man is she is married to, who are these people he comes from, and in what lie these differences she feels exist between them and the community, which is supposed to be theirs but in which they have mostly been looked at and treated as outcasts, indeed, as rebels.

As to myself, I have very often reflected about the sources of
the differences that I have always clearly seen between us, Seawi
of the Forty Arpents and most of the people of the Reserve; those
sources dig deep in the history that I have come to know about
us. However, even though Bárbara's insights are not of the same
sort as mine, I am left intrigued by them and do not see them as
contradictory to my own. "You always show a special kind of
light-heartedness when we come around here," she remarked on
that last morning of our eighteen-day trip, while we were still in
Syracuse. "Your life started here, and some of your ancestors were
Onondaga and came from right here," she said, as if to resolve an
enigma she knew I have been contending with for a very long time.

Such details about my people's history and life may seem not so
significant in the history I am making but, as will become clearer
as we go on, find meaning in my way of explaining how an
ancient sense of an original Wendat identity has been preserved.
That very sense of an original Wendat identity – and Canadian
history – has all to do with how the Wendat created their reality
according to a circular and matricentric worldview. At this point,
as will be done throughout, I will do a brief recalling of the original and primary reason why I am writing this book, which I have
titled *Eatenonha*.

As you, my reader, already know, from the time I was very young
I have been instructed that similar to the other Native nations,
the way of my Wendat ancestors was to observe and recognize
the relationships that exist between all the beings of all orders in
Nature. In my life as a Wendat and in my career as a teacher and
a writer, I have found that an excellent, simple way to explain
the essential Aboriginal/Indigenous philosophy to non-initiated
folks was to name as "circular thinking" this capacity of Earth-
centred peoples to see that great, universal relationship between
all beings. This way of looking at the world stands in dialectic
contrast with "linear thinking," an expression that implies that a
society has typically lost, or is in the process of losing the capacity of imparting to its members the aptitude to see and recognize
that great circular web of relationships or, put more simply, that
keener sensitivity toward life itself. My traditional instructions

and the living examples in my social surroundings have equally made me – and many traditional thinkers that I have known – see and be desirous to explain how a circular vision is also a *matri-centric*, or *gynocentric*[4] one. Very importantly, this implies that it is illogical and illusory to think that a patricentric society can produce circular-thinking individuals or the social and political structures that will help create individuals and communities able to think and act "circularly."

One of the most central ideas that I offer in the present essay is that we are now living in a time when human beings are becoming ever more anxious (one could even say frantic) over the effects, on human and environmental health, of man's mindless, destructive ways of relating to Eatenonha (the Earth Mother). But we, as humankind, have not yet become conscious that the real cause of such disorder is that man (that is, linear-thinking man) has come to substitute himself for woman as the creator and originator of society.

To better explain this very essential idea, the following is a quote from a conversation with Bárbara and our son, Miguel, in October 2011, which inspired me in the formulation of this idea. (The conversation, as always, happened in Spanish and French.) "To be viable, a society must place man in such a way as to let him see the feminine nature as the observable manifestation of the laws of life and of the universe. A non-viable society is one where man builds for himself a material, political power that makes him see himself as the source of an order to be created and maintained by him. In such societies (the world itself has then lost its sense), woman and the feminine nature (the Earth herself) become energies to be harnessed and transformed, always violently, into masculine power. Man becomes condemned to be an emasculated, pathological version of himself. Life's intended protector has become life's destroyer." Our goal, for now and for our collective future, is to create a country, Canada, and a world where individuals will be able to see themselves as sons, daughters, and relatives of their Mother Earth, of their Eatenonha.

Let us go back to our examination of the historical roots of the Seawi, now a francicized family name (*Sioui*) but originally a people who formed a branch of one of the Five Nations of the Wendat Confederacy or possibly a branch of a nation having once composed another politically related Confederacy, such as the Erie, for example. To us, the descendants of the original Seawi, and to the specialists of our history, our name is essentially and perennially associated with the role of defence. All of our Chiefs of old bore the title (in European languages) of "War Chief" or "Chef de Guerre," which to us would be more accurately rendered as "Chief of Defence,"[5] or "Chief of External or International Affairs." As is also well known by historians, Headmen such as Michel Tsioui Teashiandareh, one of the four Wendat Chiefs who was received by King George IV in 1825, had the dual function of Chief of the Warriors and Keeper of the Wampums (elaborate belts of sacred beads made from seashells that served as registers of agreements and treaties concluded between Nations).

Until now, no one has been able to establish beyond doubt the origin of the name Seawi. As is the case for all societies who traditionally have not known the need to develop Western-style literacy, it is often impossible to meet the standards of conventional history in its quest for unassailable, scientific truth. Indigenous/ Aboriginal people, who incarnate and live their own history in both flesh and spirit, are primarily interested in knowing and understanding the living feeling of their ancestors, present in their Elders, about that history. It is in this that lies the difficulty for these two parties – the Indigenous and the "specialists" (sometimes called "Indianists") – to come to terms and to collaborate in creative, mutually and collectively liberating ways.

The name Seawi has many renditions and spellings in English, in French, as well as in various Iroquoian languages (we will see further on why I also use the term *Nadowek*). Possibly the very first appearance of the name in the historical records is in the *Jesuit Relations* of 1653. This is four years after the final dispersion of the Wendat Confederacy. Other allied Confederacies had also been vanquished and dispersed, mostly through epidemics of European origin and through the superior Dutch-supplied firepower of the Hodenosaunee. These Nations and Confederacies included the Neutral Confederacy, who originally had an even larger population than the Wendat, the Tionontati (Tobacco Nation), the Erie (People of the Cougar), and others who were less well known, which together may have numbered as many as 200,000 individuals. The Five Nations (Hodenosaunee), in their need to stop the quickly mounting power of the French (and not out of a natural killing instinct, as many textbooks still teach Canadian children), were thus able to save themselves from extinction by either coercing or persuading the hopelessly battered, reduced peoples and remnants of Confederacies to join them by "becoming Iroquois." This allowed these peoples to survive, admittedly in a different social and cultural form but, nevertheless, survive as matricentric, circular thinkers and avoid the deleterious, colonial brainwashing that so adversely and frequently affected so many Indigenous peoples, here and around the world. Let us retain here that this rare feat of survival is to be attributed in very important measure to the superior viability possessed by matricentric, circular-thinking societies because of their ability to see and look beyond apparent differences (physical and otherwise) in peoples and individuals.

We are informed in the *Jesuit Relation* of 1653 that a last-ditch, desperate, defensive action was being mounted by an allied force of the remnants of the Nadowek (Iroquoian) Confederacies, the Neutral, the Erie, the Wendat, the Susquehanna, the Tionontati, as well as numerous traditional allies, such as the Algonquin, the Nipissing, the Odawa, the Potawatomi, and many other Algonquian Nations. The aim of that force of about 2,000 men was to safeguard the immemorial socio-political order that had existed in their vast region of the Northeast. The leader, possibly an Erie or a Wendat according to the Jesuits, was named Achawi. The form of that name closest to this Jesuit rendition is to be found in the Onondaga name *Hosahawi*. This name is given by that Nation as another rendition for Seawi, the name that was taken out of the roll call of the Onondaga Civil Chiefs in the 1880s.

Based on what I know about the history and the social ways of my people and all of our Amerindian congeners, I think it is entirely possible that at the conclusion of that war, lost by Achawi and the allied Nations, that that leader was offered, and accepted, a seat at the Confederate Council of the Hodenosaunee and that many of his followers chose to integrate under him as a new segment of that Confederacy, possibly as the Seawi. It is also entirely plausible that these adoptees were the "offspring" that the Onondaga of the 1880s were still referring to, even though the events leading to their joining the Hodenosaunee would have occurred 230 years or so before.

There continues to be a debate among the Hodenosaunee traditionalists about the eventual removal (in the 1880s) of the name Seawi from the Onondaga roster of Condoled Chiefs.[6] Some say that the Confederacy thus returned to the original number of forty-nine Civil Chiefs. Others maintain that the Peacemaker, Deganawidah – the originator of the Hodenosaunee – envisioned and decreed that the Confederacy Council would be composed of fifty Chiefs, which it was until the name Seawi was withdrawn.

There is also the strong probability that there existed a Seawi political entity before it became an "offspring" of the Onondaga Nation. Some hypothetical basis for this can be recognized in the fact that the Headman of the Hurons of Detroit, who died in 1701 at over sixty years of age, was the illustrious Wendat Kondiaronk, who is also reported to be a Soiaga. The composition of this name, with the ending *aga*, quite likely indicates a national or sub-national affiliation. The first part, *Soi*, is logically associated with the appellation Seawi, customarily misspelled by French and other European writers while the second part, *aga,* as just said, refers, to a people, or a nation. In the Wendat tradition, even after his people's and the allies' final military defeat under Achawi, Kondiaronk, also an illustrious "War Chief," continued to work and fight to maintain the pre-European political order in the lands that later saw the birth of Canada and the United States.[7] To me, recapturing this very sense of how our country was born is a first step toward finding its Native soul and spirit and thus forming a true national will to care for, protect, and love the land which gives us life, our Mother Earth, our Eatenonha. This is meant to be a central contribution of the present work. We will look deeper into this very important approach to our country's history in further sections of this book.

Concluding this section on my people's and my own identity, I feel I must apologize to my reader for asking of her, of him, maybe too much forbearance for the intricacies encountered. I do hope that I was able to sustain my reader's interest in a task with a goal to establish a person's (me) entitlement to express his own sense of historical truth in spite of a never-perfect, even arguably insufficient, set of historical proofs or data.

Coming back to Bárbara's inkling about my possible blood kinship with the Onondaga, I will say that it is most certain that some of their adoptees ("offspring") were Wendat and, also certainly, Seawi. This would also be true about any and all of the nations of the greater northeastern region: our conflicts were centrally motivated by the possibility of capturing and adopting most of our captives (some, of course, were "thrown in the fire" (burned at the stake) in order to atone for otherwise irreparable offences suffered by one's Clan and Nation). These conflicts (the word *war* would not convey their true purpose and meaning) are called *mourning wars* in the anthropological discourse, and in the analysis that we are developing in this present text, can only occur in a matricentric context. Typically, patricentric societies make war in order to terminally vanquish, or eliminate, their enemies. Again, we are touching on the most central point of this essay: circular-thinking/matricentric societies *alone* can generate ideas, social mechanisms, and lifeways that allow for imparting the proper sensitivity for life and all the orders of beings that compose it. (As we shall see further on, the Clan Mothers' authority was very present in the military domain, even especially so.)

Also, as previously illustrated in our reference to the life and work of Wendat Headman Kondiaronk, we find evidence in the primary documents of close political affiliation between the Wendat and the Onondaga. In his *Histoire de l'Amérique Septentrionale*, published in 1753, French historian Bacqueville de la Potherie informs us that in 1699, Paul Tsieweioui (quite probably the *Royaner* bearing the name Seawi), Chief Orator of the Iroquois of Mount Royal (an amalgam of refugees from many nations) was travelling in a delegation to Quebec City. We know that the Onondaga are, in the Hodenosaunee, the Keepers of the Central

Fire and, as such, that Chief Paul Tsieweioui had very important functions. We also have in mind that it now would have been forty-six years (1699) since the adjunction of the name Seawi to the Onondaga roll call of Civil Chiefs (Condoled Headmen). I have long asked myself (like some others among my people) why and at what time we, the refractory Huron of the Forty Arpents Reserve, had elected to establish ourselves there, at a convenient distance from the double missionary and governmental control that was the rule in the Reserve of Village-des-Hurons and against the will of Church and State. The same Church and State who, from the moment we began to occupy that small territory, did their utmost to destroy our community. In 1904, they succeeded when our Reserve was sold with the complicity of the government-appointed leaders of Village-des-Hurons and with the blessing of the religious authorities – without compensation to the ones who lost their livelihood, their independence, indeed, their future as a community. Were the Hodenosaunee, through this delegation, attempting to establish or reinforce an outpost of the League out there, close to the headquarters of the colonial government in Quebec City? Were the Onondaga Seawi and the other (Wendat) Seawi working together to help the Hodenosaunee achieve these common strategic goals? I have thought to place around that time the moment of the beginning of our Forty Arpents community, lost, as I said, about two hundred years later. For a long time, I and others have felt and expressed sorrow and sadness at how hard a fate was thus created for us through our coming there, amid such a culturally and ideologically adverse environment, so far from our real kin, Hodenosaunee, Wyandot, Algonquians, and others. "Why don't we go back home?" my mother told me many times,[8] with a nostalgia born of the hopelessness that this could ever come true.

This expression of sadness and loss must not imply that we, Wendat, are and have been strangers or squatters in our lands, now situated in the Province of Quebec. "You [Hurons] should show gladness and gratitude that the French gave you a Reserve in New France so that you could be saved from total extermination at the hands of your Iroquois enemies," a Québécois

Jesuit condescendingly objected to my mother during a radio interview on the film *Blackrobe*, then premiering in Canadian cinemas. "Are you meaning that you people arrived here in our country with land in your haversacks?" was Dr Éléonore Sioui's succinct reply. I have, for my part, dedicated a chapter of my first book (*For an Amerindian Autohistory*) as a refutation of that perverted argument historically used by Quebec to deny the Wendat their rights in this new political entity created on their land and now called "Quebec." That sadness expressed by my mother was not a denial of our rights to our ancestral domains situated in present-day Quebec: she was voicing our traditional people's pain of having come back to part of their former homeland, the area of Quebec City, and failing to create for themselves a home and a future (on the small territory of the Forty Arpents). My mother was expressing the grief felt by many of the traditional Wendat, most of them Seawi, of having heroically fought and lost a long, cruel battle, because their former domains (the original Kanatha[9]) had become completely overtaken by the invading French.

THE 1904 DISPERSAL:
LIFE IN VILLAGE-DES-HURONS

Though it is not my purpose in this essay to give a history of the existence and the struggle of the Seawi community of the Forty Arpents, it is indeed necessary, in view of our main objectives, to properly instruct my readers as to the specific worldview that animated the community[10] and that it ceaselessly and keenly fought to preserve.

At the time of the dislocation in 1904, almost all the families living on the Forty Arpents used the surname Sioui. It can be surmised that women from outside the group were integrated through marriage or otherwise, and that the people progressively abandoned the ancestral clan system. It can also logically be suggested that since the whole community traced common clan affiliations to the Seawi branch of the Wendat (or the Onondaga, or some other Hodenosaunee Nation), the name Seawi, in one form or another, came to be used as a European-style (patriarchal) family name. However, the rich documentation left by members of the group, especially leaders, mostly men but also women, shows that their manners of government, right until the final dispersal in 1904, continued to be markedly traditional, which means in the terminology proposed in this book, circular and matricentric.[11] One of the most striking features revealed in that documentation is the remarkable discursive power possessed by these leaders and by many of their fellow community members. One can easily see that this community was keenly aware of the power of words and of speech and that, in spite of limited accessibility to books, documents, and schooling, it quite deliberately sought to deepen its knowledge of the things it needed to be mindful and cognizant of for its self-defence and survival.

"The Sioui of the Forty Arpents are bad Hurons," was the verdict pronounced by the Reserve missionaries, speaking of their poor attendance at mass and other religious services. "The Siouis still have savage ways, they are fanatics and heretics," was the common thinking of many of the folks on the main Reserve according to my grandmother Caroline. My grandmother recalled that this categorization of the Sioui of the Forty Arpents had become more firmly implanted and more discriminatory after Stanislas Sioui, the Headman of the Forty Arpents community at the time prior to the final dispersal in 1904, renounced his Catholic faith to become Presbyterian in a dramatic effort to gain federal support for his people in their quest to be recognized as a distinct "Indian Band." Stanislas Sioui declared that as a Chief of his people, whom the British Crown had the fiduciary responsibility to protect, he "must belong to the same religion as his King."

For many decades, as the dislike for and disapproval of the existence of the Forty Arpents Indians grew,[12] the main effort of that community's leadership was to persuade the federal government and the public at large that it had as strong (if not stronger) an entitlement as did the Hurons of the main Reserve to be federally recognized as a "Band" in its own right.

MORE HISTORY OF THE SEAWI OF
THE FORTY ARPENTS RESERVE

As previously stated, one of the ultimate goals that I pursue is to explain how a rare, authentic sense of Canadian history has been preserved within a minute surviving portion – the Seawi – of a once very large and powerful Aboriginal Confederacy, the Wendat.

In trying to preserve their existence as a political and cultural entity, the Seawi were facing odds that were simply insurmountable. Church and State were in league against them, as they were against the cultural survival of any and all Native people, and it was only a matter of time before they were dislocated and very likely dispersed, once and for all, as the last free remnant of the former Wendat Confederacy. That fated outcome came in 1904.[13] These sorts of stories about dispossessing Aboriginal people are only too familiar: some politician made the promise that, should he be favoured at the upcoming provincial election, he would "get the savages out of those lands," lands that many settlers were coveting. Such is the account passed down to us by our older people. Those Elders also recalled that the ones to be dislodged (twenty families or so), were also "promised" the sum of six dollars per head, which, at any rate, was never paid out. Predictably, through foul play and scheming, the Reserve authorities, hand-picked by the governments of the day, were able to have their way, thus crushing the dream that a proud, lively, promising Indian community would continue to exist.

Most of the families were of scarce financial means but, with the meagre handouts dispensed by the federal government to on-Reserve Status Indians and through the support of relatives already living on the Reserve, managed to make the transition to their new life. That was the case of my paternal great-grandfather's family, as this ancestor drowned accidentally while working as Chief-guide for a team of forest surveyors. His son, my grandfather Paul, also a renowned woodsman, preferred not to talk about the Forty Arpents swindle, or even about his life in the forests. When pressed by his grandsons to recount some of the exploits he was known for among the other great hunters of the day, he would say something like "the best thing for you to do is to work well in school," which left us completely baffled.

Some other displaced families headed for the wider world and became part of the Huron diaspora (we did not use the term *Wendat* then), both in Canada and the US. Inspired by their ancestors' enterprising spirit, many became successful in a variety of domains, from business to arts, to sports, and to science and education. But the hardship and injustice experienced by the Forty Arpents Siouis had long-lasting consequences. Evidently, the integration of many of those families into the federally recognized community of Village-des-Hurons (then often called Indian Lorette) was a thing almost impossible to realize. Many of the new residents were wont to express their anger at the government and at the conniving Band Council. What made the whole scene even more revolting was the fact that several non-Aboriginal families had recently been given "Indian status" by these same authorities – a move that was regarded by the dispossessed Siouis as a despicable, inhumane manoeuvre to offset any demographic weight they might still have had when the time came for any "democratic" decision to be taken concerning them. Understandably, the warning often uttered publicly by many successive Reserve politicians was to never elect any Siouis (clearly meaning the ones who came from the former Forty Arpents) to any public office, for they will "throw the adoptees back out of the Reserve." It would take no less than eight decades before any of the Sioui descendants of those families could be elected on the National Council on the basis of a traditionally oriented political program. A monetary settlement of twelve million dollars was allotted in 1999 for the loss of those lands. However, no mention was ever made, anywhere or in any form, of those who had constituted the community of the Forty Arpents Reserve. To underline the need felt by the present-day authorities to not risk stirring up old feelings, not a word has ever been spoken publicly about this historical injustice; that is, the history of why that compensation was eventually granted to the present-day Huron-Wendat community, the majority of who remain uninformed about an important episode in their history.

As has begun to be shown in this essay, the essential, historic quest of the traditional Wendat, of which we have said the Forty Arpents people were the last free remnant, came to be invested in my maternal family. It should be noted that I am limiting myself, in the present book, to looking at our political existence in Canada, and not North America-wide. It is important and interesting to note here that the Forty Arpents Siouis still clung to a matricentric ideology in their society at the time of their dispersal. Therefore, their men went far and wide to find and marry women of varied, often non-Aboriginal origins and, consequently, we did not have the problems of excessive consanguinity frequently experienced by small communities in the father-centred society. With this, I wish to explain that even though we (the people of that community) recognized our strong, common roots as Hurons, we still hung on to our ancestral lifeways (circular and woman-centred) because this allowed us to live by values that we knew and felt were our own. Our men and women were thus formed from an early age in the knowledge of what leadership was about and what was expected and needed from a leader. (We will discuss more on the theme of leadership in matrilineal/matricentric societies further on.)

We have briefly taken note of the role and character of leaders such as Stanislas, Éléonore, and Emery Sioui. We will now look in some depth at the life and the ideology of two of the leaders just named – Emery, the last Chief of the remnant of his community, and his daughter, my mother, Dr Éléonore Sioui. As well, we will briefly highlight the life and work of a very important leader, arguably one of the most determining Aboriginal political actors of the twentieth century in Canada, Jules Sioui. Once more, my aim in presenting to you a story so close to my personal and family histories, dear reader, is only tangentially to expose a rather common example of how the original peoples of Canada were dispossessed. My primary aim is to show to you, as Canadians, and to the world, that there is something much more important and essential than the mere consciousness of their victimhood that the First Peoples have wished and continue to wish to preserve and share with their fellow countrypeople and the world: it is the sense of how their ancestors, their people, have elaborated ways and principles to relate to the land and to all the beings that make up the life to be lived from it and with it. Like all traditional Aboriginal people, the Siouis of the Forty Arpents have used their own particular gifts to carry on, in a new context, the quest of their ancestors to keep alive the view of life and the sense of history that they have imparted to the world, as we all must survive and be happy and secure while we are making this beautiful journey on and with our Mother Earth, our Eatenonha.

EMERY AND ÉLÉONORE SIOUI

Emery Sioui, born in 1888, grew up listening to the adults and the Elders of his community speak about and discuss their struggle against the governments, about his people's ideology, and about why and how they must stay alive. Among his teachers were the likes of Stanislas Sioui, often spoken of as a "heretic" by authorities and the common folk of the Lorette Reserve; Thomas Sioui, another vocal leader, son of Chief Michel Tsioui Teashiandareh who was one of the four Huron Chiefs hosted by King George IV in April 1825, and known for the discussions he had with sociologist Léon Gérin; and Elizabeth Sioui, a highly respected Clan Mother, leader, and strategist of the Forty Arpents.

My grandmother Caroline Dumont told me that her husband, like many men in all epochs, had hoped their first child would be a boy. It was, however, Éléonore who arrived instead. To better speak of the absolute fondness of my grandfather for that daughter, as well as to illustrate the type of guidance and education she received from her father, I will give here an excerpt from a text that I presented in June 2013 at the North American Indian Studies Association (NAISA) where a former master's student of mine, Dr Kathryn Magee Labelle, now a professor at the University of Saskatchewan, directed a panel dedicated to the life and work of Dr Éléonore Sioui. My paper was titled: "Éléonore Sioui Tecumseh."

The panel's presentations were by Kathryn Magee Labelle (University of Saskatchewan), Chief Jan English (Wyandots of Kansas), Clifford E. Trafzer (a spiritual son of my mother, a Wyandot, and a Distinguished Professor at the University of California Riverside), and myself (University of Ottawa).

My presentation:

Dear friends and relatives,

It is for me a great joy to be here in Saskatchewan, a province of kind, friendly people who once welcomed me and my family with open arms and heart, a place that still feels like home. It is also the place where I had my most significant, transformative experiences as an educator and as a person. Thank you again, Saskatchewan and its peoples! And today, thank you to the University of Saskatchewan for hosting this wonderful and very important annual NAISA Conference. Finally, many thanks to my former MA student at the University of Ottawa, Kathryn Magee Labelle, now become my colleague as a professor at this university, a woman whom I much admire for her integrity and courage. Katie, even though she never met my mother, has had the keenness of mind and spirit to want to bring Dr Éléonore Sioui, Wendat scholar, speaker, and social activist, more fully and centrally to the attention of the academy and of the world at large.

Éléonore Sioui was born on 20 May 1920 and returned to the spirit world in March 2006. My mother was the first daughter born to Caroline Dumont and Emery Sioui. My maternal grandmother, a Huron, often expressed her pride in being the "cousin" of Gabriel Dumont, the renowned defender of the Métis and Indian peoples out West and one of the foremost comrades-in-arms of the celebrated Métis leader Louis Riel. Like her own mother, Éléonore Gros-Louis, my grandmother became a medicine woman who people of all walks of life and origins, both local and from far

and wide, came to visit and consult about all the problems
that affect us humans, including physical health.

Éléonore Sioui's father was one in a long, continuous line of
Seawi leaders. Emery Sioui was the last Chief of the Wendat
(Hurons) of the Forty Arpents, that small community that
claimed to be Canada's last authentic community descended
from the original Wendat Confederacy and that, for 160
years, had put up a heroic fight against Church and State to
be allowed to survive in its small territory, situated about
twenty kilometres north of the city of Quebec. That last
dispersal of the traditional Wendat is a sordid story and the
final act of a long, yet unacknowledged genocide. That dispersal took place in 1904 and most of the twenty or so families,
thus rendered destitute, had no choice but to move onto the
main Reserve of Village-des-Hurons (now renamed Wendake)
where their history of resistance made them be seen and
treated as a threat by the government-appointed authorities
and by many in the populace. Some families somehow managed to remain on their former land. The federal government,
in its well-known benevolence toward the ones it has dispossessed, accorded them a seat at the Council of the only Huron
Reserve it recognized, Village-des-Hurons, where most of their
relatives would henceforth reside. The government abolished
that seat in 1935. Emery Sioui was its last holder. He died at
forty-eight, three years later.

Emery Sioui's dream as an Indian and as a Wendat leader
was far bigger than of obtaining justice for his dismembered,
dispossessed people. When Éléonore was born, her father so
much admired her beauty and intelligence that he saw in her
one destined to be a great leader. And so, Chief Emery Sioui
set out to dutifully and caringly raise his first child as the
one who was going to lead the ancestral fight of their people.
However, following the way of the Wendat, a people central in
pre- and post-European trade and politics, this struggle was to
continue to be inclusive of all peoples, Native and non-Native.
Like all traditional First Nations people, the Wendat, from the
first moments following the Europeans' arrival, conceived of

their responsibility as original peoples to assume their role as leaders in their own land, which meant teaching their newly come human relatives how to live in this land in a socially and environmentally conscionable, intelligent manner. Such was the kind of leader Emery Sioui was and such is the way Éléonore was taught how to lead.

Emery Sioui was an acknowledged, successful hunter and trapper. The oldest child of his family and with an ailing father, he began working like a man at the tender age of nine, cutting and selling firewood and helping his mother wash and deliver the clothes of well-to-do people of nearby localities. When, toward the age of forty, his own health began to leave him, Emery taught himself how to read both French and English. His fascination was biology. Learned people who knew him told me that he was a born, self-taught biologist. Chief Emery Sioui began to build up a world-class fur business. His breeds of minks and foxes became known beyond our country's borders as among the world's best. My grandfather imported wagonloads of old and wounded horses from this here province of Saskatchewan to feed his beautiful, precious fur-bearing animals. His fur-ranching business was very successful until wartime came and quickly and utterly destroyed his enterprise, based on the production of luxury goods. Emery Sioui died soon after from diabetes and exhaustion.

Long before this heart-breaking end to their ranching enterprise, however, Emery Sioui and Caroline Dumont had well established themselves as an important social presence amid the settler population around this new parish of Saint-Gérard Magella, which, as just seen, had been created from an act of dispossession committed against the Siouis. Caroline Dumont, besides being a keen business associate to her husband, was a most respected and sought-after healer and the midwife who attended to the birth of nearly all the children of these families of newcomers. Consequently, that grandma of mine, who played such a crucial role in my own upbringing, was revered by everyone, white and Indian alike. Emery Sioui, as to him, was for all those years a provider of employment, food, and

other necessities of life for anyone in need. Seventy-five years
after his passing, he is still talked about in those parts as a
man of extraordinary generosity, kindness, and courage. Such
was the social and family setting in which Éléonore Sioui was
born and raised.

An infinite pride in her own people moved my mother. Her
every feeling, her every action was the product of a sovereign knowledge that she was a carrier of the true, living,
immensely rich, and beautiful civilization of this land, the
land of her First Nations people. As a proud Wendat, she was
deeply convinced that the whole effort of an Indian had to be
of keeping and exercising a role of leader in his/her land, in
every respect, whether it be spiritual, intellectual, political, or
cultural. And so, there was neither time nor reason to linger
on feelings of victimization. She trained everyone around her
to be a leader and a teacher. She could be and often was very
hard and tough in her ways of touching people's hearts but,
quite generally, her deep personal conviction quickly and
surely gained people to her cause, her people's cause – the
cause, as she often said, of helping to heal not just people, but
the world as a whole.

Deep down in her soul, my mother's conviction and pride
came from a sharp, vivid pain, which she, as a Wendat, felt for
what she often named the genocide of her people. The deep
hurt was compounded by the monstrous gigantic lie contrived
by Canada's early missionary historiographers, still repeated
and used today, about how the destruction of our peoples
occurred. My mother belonged to a people who have never
believed in the social and historical mythology invented by
the invading elites and she suffered accordingly. The Wendat
had been the most central Aboriginal Confederacy in eastern North America. Their destruction through biological
warfare, as well as through political intrusions and manipulations, meant the beginning of the final dismantlement of
the Aboriginal socio-political order and the beginning of the
creation of this new country named Canada, admittedly the
world's best and most beloved country, though to its First

Peoples still often a very harsh, soulless place to exist in. In a global historical context, once the great Eastern Aboriginal Confederacies – the erstwhile bulwark of the First Nations of Canada – were destroyed and gone, the Indian Residential Schools and other sordid genocidal contrivances were just tragedies waiting to happen.

I have just given an insight into the roots of Éléonore Sioui's moral pain for our loss as a Nation and as a Confederacy. I now wish to give my view of her strategy as a woman spirit-warrior. Like her parents and her ancestors before her, my mother's prime purpose was, as previously alluded to, to use the vision and the spiritual medicine of her people in order to help heal a world already sick and getting sicker by the moment. For that purpose, she saw the need to enlist the help, strength, and power of all people, the whole human family, while acknowledging and affirming the primary role to be played by the First Nations people. This is where I touch on the most central tenet in her philosophy: that for any healing to be possible, the woman must return to the central place she once occupied in our nations. My mother, like many sages, believed and said that as long as man uses force to place himself at the centre of all his man-made world and its organizations, the only result to be expected is abuse, strife, dysfunction, violence, and degradation of the natural forces that give and sustain life in all its forms.

A Wendat, Éléonore Sioui was heiress to a matrilineal and matricentric worldview. Not all First Nations societies are, or have been matrilineal, but all have been and most continue to be and think matricentric. In such societies, in the words of our adopted clan-relative and world-renowned ethnohistorian Bruce Graham Trigger, it was impossible for a man to abuse or mistreat his spouse, or women, generally.[14] It is through ideological brainwashing (a phenomenon often called "education"), thought Éléonore, that we have come to live in communities and in a society where violence against women – and against the Earth, the ultimate feminine being – is so widespread, so pervasive.

Éléonore grew up in a family where women were still
regarded with very high respect, never knew mistreatment
at the hands of their menfolk, and often had first say in any
and all matters of importance to family and community. In
this also, leaders such as Emery Sioui showed a clear and
eloquent example. Observing this principle accords with the
saying often heard among our Hodenosaunee (Iroquois) kin:
In all your important community actions, always listen very
carefully and respectfully to the voices of the women and you
will thus never fail. Whenever we have not done this, we have
always failed. Our mother and leader, Éléonore, ingrained in
all our spirits the reality that women have the power to create
societies – they know the price and the value of life because
they conceive and give birth to us. They are the ones who
teach us the reasons why we have to have compassion, empathy, and solicitude for others and for all other-than-human
beings. Therefore, allowing women to have and take their
place at the centre of our communities and societies is much
more than an act of justice: it is an irreplaceable strategy for
our global survival. That is certainly something that I learned
from my mother.

Éléonore Sioui married a man of her own people. My
father, Georges-Albert Sioui, was the son of Paul Sioui, a great
hunter, guide, and store owner whose widowed mother had,
like many other dispossessed Siouis of the Forty Arpents,
resigned herself to make a life with her children on the main
Reserve where they had had no choice but to relocate. This
meant that my father, though a very proud Indian and Wendat
at heart, did receive the normal, ordinary brainwashing that
came with learning how to be a "good" Reserve Indian, who
never shows or says that he thinks things ought to be different
than they are. In other words, my father, though consciously
a dispossessed, dislocated man like many folks of his generation, knew how to put on a happy front – he was a good
Huron and a good Indian, he even was a good Sioui. Most
importantly, he was, as I will say further on, "a quiet rebel
and a matriot."

There was, of course, a sombre underside to my father's happy appearance. A good Reserve Indian never questioned Church or State – at least openly – but that good Reserve Indian, especially one from a freshly dispossessed family, was one repressing a lot of feelings of anger and humiliation. For that particular pain of the soul, society has a common remedy: alcohol. Alcohol does, that is certain, numb the pains felt in the soul, but does so at a very high cost. While it allows bearing an otherwise unbearable life condition, it takes away from self and, eventually, from the social environment the sensitivity about life, which, as we said a moment ago, women naturally and instinctively produce in their role as the main creators of society. This means that women – and the children they bear – are alcohol's (and drugs') first and principal victims.

Yes, Éléonore, like so many of her Aboriginal and non-Aboriginal sisters, had to cope with a married life marred by the almost constant presence of alcohol and violence. Yes, the man whom I personally loved and admired so much was able to abuse and mistreat the one human being that I have loved above any other in my life, my mother. However, this presentation is not meant to be a recounting of my own, or of my family's history; this presentation is a narration of our universal First Nations and human history, through the lived experience of one First Nations woman, Éléonore Sioui. How did a woman like her, a leader trained in her own ancestral tradition, deal with this condition that is so much a common fact of life for our people, for our women?

Éléonore Sioui was pre-destined to single-handedly challenge and help transform a system that had been thought out by the invading social and religious elites to absolutely and radically crush the life out of the First Nations of the land, a system that worked with terrible efficiency. First, a poor, lone woman had to face up to the triumvirate which managed every orderly Reserve in those days not-too-distant: the Indian agent, the priest, and the Indian affairs-appointed Chief. And regarding that concept of order, our Reserve

was a shining model, which government and church were
always proud to display for anyone. To make a very long
story shorter, my mother, inspired by her father's own efforts
to educate himself and his insistence on the importance of
knowledge and its acquisition, chose to engage her adversaries
on the topic of education, more precisely, equal accessibility to
education for both boys and girls, women as well as men.

I was quite young, but I vividly remember that this daring
proposition coming from one of those "untamed Siouis of the
Forty Arpents" was received as an affront by the authorities
and their quite numerous sympathizers. Much worse than that,
I remember that not long after, as my mother had taken to
the habit of going to every Band Council meeting and "asking
too many questions," there came the news in our home that
the authorities wanted to have our mother checked for mental
sanity. Years later, I heard her relating to people that she was
convened to an appointment with a psychiatrist. "I just knew,"
she said, "that if I set one foot into that office, they (my enemies) would have a hold on me and my life would be finished.
They would have placed all of my [at that point, all of us seven]
children away in foster homes."

At the time this all happened, (or was prevented from
happening), Éléonore Sioui had only completed grade seven.
We saw her studying for the longest time, maybe eighteen
years in all, and working at jobs at the same time, raising
us seven children mostly alone, with the sole material and
spiritual support of her mother, my so dear grandmother
Caroline. In 1988, Éléonore Sioui became the first Amerindian
woman to graduate with a PhD in First Nations philosophy
and spirituality. What pride she instilled in so many of us!
What an example of courage and determination she set for
all of us, from whatever background we may be. And she, at
times, liked adding a funny commentary to that episode of
her life. With a glitter in her eye, she would recount that some
of her "best" former detractors would sometimes meet her
haphazardly and, of course, awkwardly risk congratulating
her on that achievement: "Hi, Éléonore. Congratulations on

obtaining your PhD." To which she would retort, "I'm sorry, for you, it will not be Éléonore, it will have to be *Doctor* from now on."

Now, to conclude, through this presentation I have wanted, my dear relatives and friends, to offer you a glimpse into the life of a very proud Wendat woman. I have meant to illustrate for you that respect and love of one's tradition and roots can lead anyone to physical, mental, emotional, and spiritual liberation and to a life of enrichment and openness and admiration for all peoples, all knowledge, all wisdom, all life.

The daughter of a Huron-Wendat hunter and traditional leader, Éléonore Sioui's life journey took her from her humble place of birth to the highest realms of Canadian and world society. In our community of Wendake, she created the Kanatha Centre for Amerindian Culture and Spirituality in the early 1970s, the first of its kind in the country, which for six years produced the magazine *Kanatha*. The centre itself continued to operate until Éléonore went from this world in 2006. For a lifetime of remarkable Aboriginal ideological leadership and constructive social activism at all levels, including international, Dr Éléonore Sioui was awarded the Medal of Officer of the Order of Canada in 2001.[15] However, even though she carried that honour with very high pride, she was wont to say that the honour most precious to her heart ever bestowed on her was the Tom Longboat Medal, which she received from our Mohawk relatives, the Chiefs of Kahnawake and Kanesatake, in 1990, for her brave, outspoken support during the Oka crisis.

Dr Éléonore Sioui will, in future times, also be remembered for her contribution to the literary and the scholarly realms. Her thinking, her ideas, she used to say, were her own people's medicine and her most profound aim was to help heal the world. As a woman of her Wendat tradition, Éléonore Sioui intimately saw and felt the needs and the pain of her First Nations people; she also saw and perceived their potential contributions to the larger society and to the world. She very clearly saw her duty to uphold that vision as something sacred. Not only did she never believe in or conform to the social mythology of the linear, patricentric world that engulfs us all, but even more importantly, she lived and thought out her destiny and that of her people according to the rights, responsibilities, and status which she knew her people's own ideology conferred on her.

I would like to leave you, my very dear friends and relatives, with two poems by her that will explain why she took on the name Tecumseh and will also give you a glimpse of the spirit in which she created and operated her International Amerindian Cultural and Spiritual Centre. Over the years, Éléonore became very inspired by the vision and life of Shawnee Chief Tecumseh, mostly because he upheld the principle of the total integrality of all the lands of all First Nations and because of his deep veneration for motherhood and for womanhood. And so, she eventually renamed her centre The Tecumseh Indian Spiritual Centre. First, here is the poem she wrote to the memory of Chief Tecumseh:

"TECUMSEH"

Only the silent night
Softly spreads the perfume
Of the autumn leaves
And the wind sings its requiem
On the solitude of his tomb
No tombstone
No sign of its place
Secret jealously kept
By his Brothers
Who still cry over the loss
Of America's greatest hero

And, finally, the poem she wrote for her Centre:
Vision for the realization of the
Tecumseh Spiritual Centre

Vision of a reunited Nation
Based on the recognition
Of its spiritual, cultural and political legacy
Through the Tecumseh Spiritual Centre
To the whole world

My people battered
With old educational concepts
Taken from a bible of blinded faith
Towards a new world envisioning love
Long ago when I was very young
I saw my people reunited again
Living healthy physically and spiritually
On our bounteous Mother Earth
Holding hands and heads held high
Adorned with Eagle Feathers
Proud, brave and courageous
Breathing freedom once again

My dear friend and relatives, I thank you for having listened to my words.

JULES SIOUI

Jules Sioui was born on 3 August 1903, one year before the forced
exodus of his parents and his community from the small territory of the Forty Arpents. Jules's immediate paternal relatives (his
mother was a French-Canadian Métis) were looked at as spiritual
leaders. According to a prophecy passed down in that lineage and
recorded in a sacred cane, Jules was to be a liberator of his people
and of all the Aboriginal people of the continent. And in the eyes
of a great many, that is really what he became.

As my purpose in this book is to trace the history of the survival of my people's worldview, and not to give a relation of the
life and work of any particular actor in that history, I will limit
myself to these very few lines about Jules Sioui. I will merely add
here that a work on the personal and political career of this very

important, though controversial, Indian leader of the twentieth
century will remain lacking until it sees the day, as I am certain it
will, sooner than later.

MY FATHER: A QUIET REBEL, A MATRIOT

The day is coming when the Indian people will cease to suffer. Time is
the Father of Truth.

Georges-Albert Sioui

There are two races of people: the kind, decent people and the unkind,
indecent people.

Georges-Albert Sioui

I have chosen these two phrases, often repeated by my father, to
begin illustrating his way of thinking about life and society. I will
also share the words of a song that I composed when he left us,
accidentally, in 1984.

> My father was a man of peace
> Who loved all people, whom all the people loved,
> He always used to say that
> Time is the Father of Truth,
> He lived a simple life
> In love with the Earth
> Mother of all people
> He wished to see as one, as true brothers
> Loving, as he was, of their Mother,
> Without frontiers or countries,
> Yes, my father believed in such a world.
> Oh! My father, you have left here,
> But your brothers know that from up there,
> Where you are, in the Land of Souls,
> On this life you have better control,[16]
> All souls are one with the Great One,

With our Creator,
Of life the Master.[17]

Georges-Albert Sioui was the offspring of a family that, by
force of circumstances, had had to make a quiet, muted transition
from its former existence on the Forty Arpents Reserve. However,
this did not mean that my father lost the sense of his people's
struggle for justice. The first son of Paul Sioui, a successful hunter
and businessman highly respected and sought after by wealthy
American visitors as a fishing and hunting guide, my father had
an early initiation about worldly manners of thinking and about
what produces influence and material affluence.[18] In that light, my
father was a Huron who was able to understand and follow the
tradition of his people, the Wendat – a people known and recognized by all, natives and newcomers, as central in the geopolitics
of the whole region of the Northeast. Thinking from their own
Eurocentric mental models, the Jesuits had observed that "the
Huron are the aristocracy of the land." As we shall see further
on, as the original peoples of this land we had an opposite view
about how human societies evolve and ought to be categorized.
It, again and always, has to do with an ability to see reality and
life in a circular manner; more concretely, it is about the degree
to which a society can impart to its members sensitivity for the
existence and the right of other-than-human beings to simply be.

To illustrate my father's ideology and briefly speak about his
life, I have chosen to present to you, dear readers and friends,
a paper I gave in 2010 at the University of Innsbruck, at a colloquium held at their University's Center for Inter-American
Studies. The theme of the colloquium was "Indigenous, National,
and Transnational Identities in the Americas."[19]

In that presentation, I propose a concept, which I
name matriotism, meant to convey the thinking and the practical
way of traditional Aboriginal people of looking at and relating
to the land, to nature. The title of my paper is "O Kanatha! We
Stand on Guard for Thee!" My main purpose is to explain how
and why we, all of us, can be "spiritual warriors" in defence of

our Mother Earth, our Eatenonha, and of all her children, both
already born and yet unborn.

"O KANATHA! WE STAND ON GUARD FOR THEE!"

*Liebe Freunde der Universität Innsbrucks, liebe Verwandten
von der Österreich und von allen Ländern, sehr beehrte
Studenten,*
    *Ich fühle mich sehr dankbar für diese Einladung von
ihrer Universität und es gibt mir grosse Freude meine liebe
Freunde, am meistens die Professorin Ursula Moser, noch
einmal zu sehen.*
I owe some of the inspiration for the title of this presentation to a late Mi'kmaq brother, a wonderfully talented singer
and song writer who has won international recognition for
his work. His name is Willie Dunn and his music has been
produced in Canada and in Germany. As a young artist, in
1969, he recorded his own version of Canada's national
anthem, "O Canada." Here is Willie Dunn's version (The
background music is a lone guitar discreetly playing the
British national anthem, "God Save the Queen"):

O! Canada, our Home and Native Land,
One hundred thousand years, we've walked upon
your sands.
With saddened hearts, we've seen you robbed and stripped
Of everything you prized.
While they cut down the trees, we were shunted aside
To the jails and the penitentiaries.
O! Canada, once glorious and free,
O! Canada, we sympathize with Thee,
O! Canada, we stand on guard for Thee.

(The guitar finishes with the first six notes of the US
national anthem.)
Some years ago, I wrote a short poem in prose in honour of
my late father. I titled that poem, to which I will come back a

little further in my talk, "Matriotism." I believe it contains the whole essence of the meaning of our Indigenous resistance to the ever-intense pressure that settler nation-states apply on us to force us to assimilate to their respective body politic. Here is my little ode to my father:

"MATRIOTISM"

I was nine years old and in fifth grade in the primary school situated in the little Québécois town just next to our Indian Reserve. A tall handsome man, standing straight as a spruce tree, attended with the other parents the monthly meeting with the teachers. He was the first Amerindian man ever hired in the Quebec provincial police, and probably in the whole country. He had come dressed in his police uniform. After the ceremony, he went to converse with the School Director. That time was the last that we, children of the Reserve, had to rise and sing "O Canada," the national anthem, a hymn in praise of our people's dispossession and consequent social misery. That man, it was you, Dad, who had so much love for our Mother Earth and taught us to respect and revere Her. *Attouget Aystan*! Thank you, my Father!

In September 2013, I published a collection of poems.[20] It contains about one hundred poems, several of which express the idea of the all-importance of Nature for us, Indigenous people. Many of those poems speak to why we not only do not wish to assimilate to settler nation-states that have been forcefully created in our territories but that we have the responsibility to indigenize, or *americize* (my own word) the ones who immigrate to our continent because without a strong connection to the Earth Mother, human beings are a hazard to Her and to all the peoples that compose Her, human and non-human.

I have thought to intersperse about half a dozen of these poems throughout my presentation today and thus make

you, dear friends, the first to publicly hear some of them.
This second poem, then, is to honour a friend of our Wendat
and Amerindian people who died in the early eighteenth
century, the Baron de Lahontan. At that early hour in the
history of our relations with the Europeans, Lahontan intimated to his colonial contemporaries that it was they who
needed to become Indians, and not the opposite. Among my
people, he is famous for his entreaty to his French congeners:
"Fais-toi Huron" (Become a Huron).

"FAIS-TOI HURON (BECOME A HURON)"

I, to become You!
To lose my soul!
To cease to feel!
My heart,
Warm abode
Of my love
For Life
Home of my own of yesterday,
Of today and of forever,
My heart to become
A mute bird
In the cold cage
Of my bones of metal?
To become You?
That must not be!
You:
Become a Huron!

Some of my people's history

My presentation to you today, dear friends, will be an exploration into the reasons why Indigenous people, generally, identify
first with their own nation and only secondarily, and sometimes
not at all, with the nation-states that have come to enclose them
and pretend to include them in their citizenry. Since I will base

this reflection on my own experience as a Wendat, I will now tell you, in brief, about what our colonial existence has been and about how my own family has evolved as a consequence of that colonial experience. My aim is to illustrate for you how the concept of *matriotism* can serve to clarify why most Indigenous people do not share the emotional ties to nation-states that most descendants of settlers in America and in other colonized parts of the world have.

Based on the poem I wrote in honour of my father, we will see why and how Indigenous people have a very different view of the history and of the human geography of their territories and their continent. We will see how this view conditions their entire worldview and thus, how they conceive of their place and role in their American universe and in the world at large with respect to all the other inhabitants (human and oth-er-than-human; material and immaterial) which make up the great, sacred Circle of Life.

I was born in 1948 to two Huron-Wendat parents in an Indian Reserve then called Village-des-Hurons, now renamed Wendake (roughly pronounced Won-da-keh), the original name of the small but strategically located country that once existed at a few hours' distance north of present-day Toronto and which the French named Huronia. Our Reserve is sit-uated about fifteen kilometres north of the city of Quebec. At the present-day location of the city of Quebec existed an Amerindian town named Stadacona. That was the town which, in 1535, the original inhabitants described to explorer Jacques Cartier as their *Kanatha*, meaning their principal town. Cartier took this information as signifying that he was then "discovering" a whole country named "Canada." The name was eventually applied to a nascent Euro-American country: Canada. For us, descendants of the original people of that region, the name *Kanatha* has kept a very important moral and symbolic significance.

My people are the descendants of the Wendat; the name Huron, which means uncouth, or ill-mannered, was the name that the French once disparagingly attached to us and that has served to justify the negation of our dignity as a people and, simultaneously, the taking of our land and our livelihood. At the time of the arrival of the Europeans, our Wendat people were one of North America's most important Aboriginal Confederacies. Similar to the Iroquois Confederacy, ours was made up of five nations. We were at the centre of quite extensive trading networks and a great number of other nations in northeastern North America utilized our language for trade and diplomacy. The Wendat Confederacy was very powerful and remarkably prosperous. The Wendat were at the heart of the Aboriginal geopolitics of the beautiful vast region which eventually gave Canada its spirit, its name, and its incomparable strength as a new country.

From a population of more than thirty thousand at the time of European arrival, only a few thousand survived the shock of very severe epidemics and a period of intense warfare, often instigated through the meddling of religious missionaries. Of these few thousand, about four hundred made their way to the vicinity of Quebec City where some of their ancestral populations had once lived until they were dispersed following the three voyages of Jacques Cartier, the so-called discoverer of Canada, and of many other French adventurers and seekers of the fabled road to the Indies. There, near present-day Quebec City, New France's authorities created a "Reserve for the settlement and conversion of the savages."

From an original location on the Île d'Orléans, within sight of Quebec's promontory of Cap-aux-Diamants, we were displaced six more times, mostly because French settlers wanted the fields that we cleared for our subsistence. Eventually, we were pushed up the foothills of the (now-called) Laurentian mountains where we have been, in our exiguous Reserve, up to this day.

I will now recite to you a poem that expresses how our people, the Wendat, were originally seen by the French and how we continue to perceive ourselves, despite sometimes being counted as extinct:

"WE ARE THE WENDAT"

"The Huron are the aristocracy,"
The French priests wrote.
We had built
And we maintained
The heart-country,
Wendake.
We were the leaders,
We were the last
Amongst the Nations,
We were
The Sastaretsi,
"Those who extend the House
To make room for ever more peoples."
We were the Wendat,
We are the Wendat.

In order to explain my ode to my father and what I mean
by the word *matriotism*, I need to give you this background
on our ancestors' history and on how this poem speaks to my
own family's history. Because of our harsh experience with
colonialism, our nation, like all Indigenous nations, is made
up of two types of people and families: those who are keenly
interested in history and ancestral values (traditionalists) and
those who are not strongly interested in these aspects of identity (progressive).

Both of my parents came from families of traditionalists.
Our way of thinking and living was characterized by a very
close connection to Nature and very high respect for our
Wendat ancestors. In our family runs rare knowledge about
plants and traditional Earth medicine. Our home life was also
marked by a strong interest in our history and, specifically,
by a pervasive, shared desire to "rewrite" our history. For the
most part, our friends and relatives were simple folks possessing little formal education but imbued with a vivid consciousness that our Wendat people, and our Indian people globally,

had been and continue to be the victims of a false, contrived non-Indigenous historiography told and written about us. A historiography that, taught and repeated in schools and in the public media over many generations, had rendered most of the Canadian citizenry unable to look at us, Indians generally, as people equally worthy of respect and, therefore, entitled like all other people to live freely, happily, and healthy in an inclusive, evolved society.

As is quite often the lot of traditionalist Indigenous people, we, a proud traditionalist Wendat family, suffered sharply and directly the effects of the cruel, racist legacy that Canadian historiography about Amerindians dealt to all Canadian citizens in all Canadian schools. Yes, as a consequence of that kind of national "education about Indians," we, as a family, were marginalized, poor, afflicted by alcoholism, and dysfunctional, but all in all, proud and thankful to the Great Spirit of Life that we were Wendat and Indian.

Here is a poem which I have dedicated to a great Cree artist from Piapot Reserve, Saskatchewan, my friend and the friend of very many of us around the world, Buffy Sainte-Marie. It bears the title of one of my favourite songs by Buffy:

"AMERICA, MY HOME"

I do not change
I have never changed
I will never change
I am America
I am the ecstasy before Creation
America that they hurt
America that they soil
America, my mother
America, for ever.

The notion of patriotism is foreign and disturbing to the Amerindian mind as it challenges the ancestral Indigenous moral precept that what many non-Aboriginal people call "their home and native land" is our Mother, our Eatenonha, as our people of old used to refer to Her. To us, the word "land" can too easily evoke the idea of a commodity, that is, a thing that one can buy and sell (normally with a profit). In contrast, the expression "our Mother Earth" carries a soothing, peace-giving feeling of belonging to a big powerful, universal family of which she, the Earth, is the Mother – a Being of infinite beauty, goodness, and love for all Her children, human and other-than-human.

Whenever we, traditional Amerindians, hear the word "land" used to refer to our Mother Earth, we become worried and defensive. Because we live with this constant feeling that we must defend our Mother Earth against governments and states that have by force appropriated Her and are treating Her as their material possession, our existence as Indigenous people cannot but be a perpetual political and spiritual quest. This sense of duty permeates our hopes, our prayers, and our dreams; it is something sacred that we gently lay by our side when we go to rest at night and caringly pick up again when we wake up. Traditional Indigenous people are forced to try and live in a spiritual manner, that is to constantly acknowledge and honour, in their hearts and souls, the infinite web of sacred relations uniting all beings around the Great Circle of Life.

Indigenous people in the Americas, and probably the world over, strongly believe in their duty to affirm, mostly through their songs, dances, and ceremonies, the universal relationship that makes all life one. In fact, this belief is so prevalent that it is customary to hear their spiritual leaders say that the safeguard of life itself on our Planet Earth rests with the peoples that have preserved and maintained their sense that the Earth is a Mother to be loved and revered, that is, with the Indigenous peoples. "Our customs, our beliefs," says a *máma* (Kogi spiritual leader) of Colombia, "are as a torch, as a light which illuminates the world. If that light gets extinguished, the world will darken and die. The civilized don't know it, but if it were not for us, the world would already have ended."

Over the past four decades or so, the non-Indigenous
world has conceived and expressed new respect for
Indigenous people and their traditional knowledge.
However, in order to truly connect spiritually, emotionally, and intellectually, there needs to be more awareness
among the non-Indigenous world of the deeper reasons for
Indigenous resistance to nation-states' efforts to assimilate
them. Contrary to common thinking, these reasons have
little to do with the righting of past wrongs, which, to be
sure, have been innumerable and extremely grave and will
continue to have painful and very adverse effects on the
lives and the chances of survival of a vast majority of the
Indigenous peoples of the Americas. The real, deep reason
for the stark refusal of Amerindian/Indigenous peoples to be
ideologically confounded with their non-Indigenous relatives
is their very different perception of reality.

It is in their respective perception of what is happening to
our common Mother, the Earth, that the two thought-worlds
come apart. Concurrently, it is in our ability (or inability)
to cause humanity to come together to protect Her that lies
either the risk of our knowing a future of disunity and misfor-
tune or our chance of having one of togetherness, harmony,
and security. On the one hand, the non-Indigenous world
is made to believe, by many of its intellectual, political, and
spiritual leaders, that Nature, or the environment, is through
the infinite goodness of a masculine God, a marvellously
inexhaustible amount of matters which will forever and ever
satisfy the needs and fulfill the desires of all of Planet Earth's
human inhabitants, that is, those who have the ingenious-
ness to extract from it (from her) the basic materials needed
to fabricate many of these goods that people are so often
misled to think they necessitate. On the other hand, traditional Indigenous people – and an ever-growing number of
non-Indigenous people – see, feel, hear, and smell that the
Earth, their Mother, is being ceaselessly, thoughtlessly abused
and treated violently and with spite, cut all apart into pieces
according to the fancy of powerful humans.

My father, that spring day of 1957, acted courageously and showed his loyalty to his ancestors and to his people. My father was a true and loyal son of the Earth. In that sense, he was, to use the word of the great Goethe, *ein Weltbürger* (citizen of the world), who saw that mankind had to evolve out of a narrow vision of national or ethnic-based identity. Thus, my father was able to profoundly feel that "his people" included all of humanity, as well as all the other-than-human peoples around the Great Sacred Circle of Life.

My father, that day, posed a deed of matriotism: he could not simply tolerate that his own children and others mindlessly accept to register in their conscience a hymn which was meant to strip them of their pride as Indigenous children and of their sense of their particular responsibility in relation to the Earth and the defence which we all owe Her from the fact that we are all Her children.

There was, however, a definite social risk involved in choosing the path he chose to take, especially for a man without material wealth or influence who, besides, had sworn allegiance to Her Majesty the Queen of England, then Canada's Sovereign and Ultimate Ruler. Through his public deed, my father expressed his conviction that our Mother Earth, and no one else, is the One to whom we owe our first allegiance. The Queen is a human invention; the Earth is our Mother and a living gift from our Creator, or the Universal Intelligence, or "the Great Spirit." There could be, and in fact there was, a social price to pay for publicly showing and demanding respect for beliefs so contrary and opposed to social and religious convention, especially at a time, six decades ago, when virtually no one dared publicly express such difference in belief. My father, just like our sages of old and of today, never wished to question in others a healthy, open-minded national pride, he simply and humbly believed that the first loyalty of fellow humans should rest with our common Mother Earth.

Without any practised discourse to that effect, my father based his act (of matriotism) on our Wendat and Indigenous thinking that our whole ability to live in balance, as humans,

depends on our being conscious that it is our Mother Earth
who sustains us physically, emotionally, mentally, and spiritually. To us, traditional Indigenous people, God, the Universal
Intelligence, or still, Nature, is so immensely great, wise, and
powerful that we dare not think that we can understand His/
Her thinking and motives or, in fact, that such an almighty
Being can be present to our daily wants and worries or, even
less, needs anything from us. The only thing we, humans, can
do, in relation to the Great Master of Life is to humbly and
wholeheartedly express our gratitude for the gifts constantly
received from Her/Him. In contrast, if we are attentive and
therefore believe in our Mother, the Earth, we are enabled to
carry on an intense, wonderfully inspiring, and intimate com-
munication with Her at every moment of our lives.

This is the reason why we see ourselves as matricentric (that
is, Earth-based) thinkers and that this Indigenous approach
to life is reflected in our social customs and in our ways of
constructing our societies, as well as in many of our Creation
Stories. In this reason is also found the explanation of why
traditional Amerindian, and Indigenous and Earth-centred
people in all parts of the world, vividly resist pressure to be
assimilated to mainstream socio-political and religious systems, as all of these are patriarchal and patricentric. We also
call this way of thinking and of living the Way of the Circle,
that is, the traditional Indigenous practice of recognizing and
honouring the universal web of relationships that unites all
beings of all natures, or the Great, Sacred Circle of Life. My
father was a true humanist, a spirit-warrior, as Indigenous
people so respectfully say. My father had a deep love for the
Earth. My father was a matriot.

I now wish to read to you another poem I wrote some years
ago about the way leaders are chosen and elected in so-called
modern democracies. We, Amerindians, who have given the
world real models for democracy, still possess many ideas as
to how to create true, inclusive circular (and mother-centred)
democracy.

"ELECTIONS"

The Canadians have won again
They're gonna be liberal
They're gonna be conservative
They're gonna reform
They're gonna democratize
They're gonna be sovereign
They're gonna be independant
They're gonna develop Canada,
They're gonna transform her into money, jobs.
Canada is still rich, very rich, they say.
One day, she will be poor, dirtied up,
Exhausted, sick,
Canadians will no longer be able to win, nor
Be liberal, or conservative, or democratize, or
Reform, or be sovereign, or independent.
Will there then remain someone enamoured
Of the wonderful Motherland
Strangers once named Canada?

There is only one race: the race against time

In countless Native communities in North, Central, and South
America, Indigenous people use the symbolism of the Circle
to teach and to explain their ways of knowing and of living.
Very frequently, in many parts of the entire continent, the
Circle is divided into four quarters representing the four sacred
directions, the four main elements in nature, the four dimensions of the human – the physical, the emotional, the mental,
and the spiritual – as well as many other realities as perceived
according to a general Amerindian cosmovision. Interestingly
for our present reflection, Indigenous people of the Americas
also see four families of peoples, each with its own special gift
to be shared with the three others, and the four make up one
universal human family.[21] Elders tell us that the continent of
America, where Amerindians have a position and a role of

teachers in relation to their newly arrived relatives, is the one
where humanity is in the slow process of learning that all life,
human and otherwise, is one. Our sages tell us that the time
when we are to come together as a family has arrived. We no
longer have, they say, the time to linger on our differences or
even on the wrongs that have been inflicted upon us in the past
and that we are still suffering in this so-called post-colonial
period of our history. We must concentrate on how we can use
our particular gifts and vision to mend and better the world for
everyone. We could invent and use an aphorism such as "There
is only one race: the race against time."

Daily, our Elders say to us that our Mother Earth is suffering. We all know already that the Earth is undergoing an
increasingly rapid process of deterioration through the actions
of linear-thinking humans. Here, however, I am speaking of
wise, often older human beings, in this context, Indigenous of
many nations who sometimes come to our classes and attend
our university events and tell us with genuine emotion that
they feel the pain of our Mother Earth and of the animal peoples, the bird peoples, fish peoples, plant peoples, and others.
We then receive a very rare and important kind of education,
the education of the heart, one that is largely absent in the
normal, mainstream system. We hear the voice of the Earth
and we know, with mind and heart, that it is She speaking
because She says the same things through the voices of every
one of these men and women.

Whether they be Algonquin, Ojibway, Mohawk, Innu, Inuit,
Wyandot, Cree, Mi'kmaq, Dené, Squamish, or Siksika or
whether they come from southerly climes and are Quechua,
Maya, Aymara, Nahuat, Kogi, Miskito, Mapuche, Diaguita, or
Kolla, our Elders speak with that one voice. Of course, I am,
at this moment, thinking of our venerated Algonquin Elder
William Commanda, who is ninety-six years old (he left us
one year later, in 2011) and whom some students from this
great and beautiful country of Austria have also heard when he
visited us in class and when our class visited him in his home
community of Kitigan Zibi, about an hour and a half from

Ottawa. Elder Commanda moved many to tears when he called all of us his people, his family and, using French, English, and his native Algonquin, affectionately entreated us all to turn our minds and hearts toward our Mother Earth and to be, as sons and daughters, Her spiritual guardians and defenders.

When referring to the real, deeper struggle of the Indigenous people, spiritual leaders use the expression "spiritual revolution," and by that, we generally understand three of our Indigenous historical and philosophical realities. First, the social misery that our peoples have endured as a result of colonial imposition by foreigners has been a very violent upsetting of the socio-political order that our ancestors had carefully and painstakingly elaborated in our continent over countless generations since time out of memory. Second, it has been our responsibility to restore the lost balance. Third, that in order to properly discharge this responsibility we, Indigenous people, have to think and act in accordance with our ancestral circular tradition and look at all humans (especially the ones who have come to America from other parts of the Earth to live with us) as true relatives who can and will join hands with us in this global task, vital for the future welfare of humanity.

Our peoples keep many prophecies, all of them quite similar in their practical essence: the time of mindless assault on the Mother Earth will come to an end. Signs of the arrival of that time will be plainly visible and observable in all parts of the world. That time will be one of unification of many people of all nations in defence of their common Mother Earth, their Eatenonha, and in the name of the children to be born from then up to "the seventh generations." That time will be one in which the Aboriginal Peoples of the Americas will play a central role in making humanity gain a vision of how and why life itself is but one great circle of sacred relations uniting all beings.

Matricentrism

Our Elders are equally univocal in saying to us that the world cannot begin to truly address its most critical social and

environmental challenges as long as women are not empow-
ered to return and occupy the central place where Nature has
willed them to be in their respective societies and in the global
community. At any rate, despite patriarchal and linear-thinking powers-that-be, we are beginning to see that this essential
natural dictate is being actualized. In Canada, and in many
nation-states around the world, women at times make up
the majority of students and are beginning to occupy many
positions as decision-makers in all fields of social endeavour. To our Amerindian sages, this is a very hope-giving sign
that the time of universal rebalancing, which so many of our
sages have foretold (the Incas of old have called that time the
Pachakuti) is really here; therefore, important ideas that are
Indigenous to the Americas are beginning to help refashion
the world, as foreseen by wise ancestors of old. For instance,
in classes that I and others teach in our Program of Aboriginal
Studies[22] at the University of Ottawa, I contentedly find myself
in a world drastically transformed from the one I knew as a
pupil when even a pale-faced Huron kid like myself had to
confront harsh, racist attitudes the moment some people knew
his family name, a name generally associated with Huron
and Indian traditionalism. I, therefore, say: *matricentrism* (we
could also use the word *gynocentrism*) will take us back to an
attitude of respect and love with regard to Nature, or Mother
Earth. My answer to the most pressing problems we face as
humankind is: Women of the world, get educated and you will
once again form men able to respect you as the source of their
life, and Nature herself, as the ultimate Giver of Life!

Here is a poem that speaks of the importance for the global
community of helping preserve the Indigenous languages,
therefore, the Indigenous cultures themselves:

"FIRST WORLD"

Learn as many languages as you can
To connect your heart to a common humanity.
For English, you don't have a choice,

For French and Spanish, it is strongly advisable,
For Mandarin, it may soon be a must,
For Arabic, Hindu, Portuguese and Japanese, it would be
very smart,
For German and Russian, it would show and give wisdom;
But for connecting to the beginning of time,
For learning genderlessness, racelessness, agelessness,
For thinking globally, circularly, naturally
Learn an Indigenous tongue,
Let's all do it!

The month of the Pachamáma

I then presented a short video showing glimpses of a five-week
visit I made, in 2008, to various Indigenous communities in
northern Argentina. While there, I was able to observe the
stark poverty in which these peoples live because of a particularly harsh and violent colonial legacy. However, I was
also able to witness the striking fervour and devotion of
these Amerindians to Mother Earth, whom they universally
name *Pachamáma*. Thanks to an Argentinean friend I made
in Ottawa, scholar in his own right Father Juan Domingo
Griffone, I could arrange these visits to seven different communities during the month they affectionately name *el mes
de la Pachamáma*. In most of these communities, I attended
very moving ceremonies in which the Indians, Toba, Guaraní,
Diaguita, and others, offered their Mother Earth through her
"mouth" (a hole in the ground that they reverently make and
prettily adorn) the best foods and beverages they have to offer
Her. On those occasions, they speak and express their deepest
gratitude to *Pachamáma* (Mother Earth, Eatenonha).

What I mostly learned during that trip is that, like the *Kogi
máma* of Colombia, these most gentle and humble people
harbour in their heart of hearts an invincible and ineradicable
assuredness that their spiritual ways are necessary for the main-
taining of a sacred moral order in their world and in the world
itself. Conversing and listening to them, I came to understand

that these Amerindians are acutely conscious of a responsibility that is their own of standing up for their ancestral principles and that they hold the absolute conviction that their culture and spirituality will eventually win the respect of the non-Indigenous world, for the benefit and certainly for the edification of humankind itself.

My dear friends and relatives, I would now like to end my presentation by saying how heartily I have welcomed this invitation here and how grateful I feel to the University of Innsbruck and, in a special manner, to my dear colleague and sister Dr Ursula Moser and to the Zentrum für Interamerikanischen Studien (ZIAT) for the honour of making me part of this series of lectures on Indigeneity and Identity in the Americas. Personally, I feel much hope that the ZIAT, at the University of Innsbruck, is already fulfilling one of the very important roles it has set out to have in the world: that of providing a voice to the myriad of still marginalized and oppressed Indigenous communities in America. I, personally, and in the name of my community and so many, many more, feel very thankful for this admirable and visionary undertaking. Through it, the University of Innsbruck has achieved the potential, in this truly great and beautiful country of Austria, of opening hearts in many other countries to the need of welcoming Indigenous ideas concerning how to and why encourage, promote, and find application for Amerindian sentiments on and definitions of identity and citizenship in the Americas themselves and in the world.

As a result of more than five centuries of colonial (and "post-colonial") duress, it will, for yet more time, be impossible for one whole family of peoples, that of the Americas, to come forward among the family of all peoples and make its voice heard – a voice that many people around the world are now anxious and desirous to hear, for in our global human family, no voice is negligible. We will survive and prosper all together, or not at all. In the name of my Indigenous community of the Americas, I applaud the University of Innsbruck and the Zentrum für Interamerikanischen Studien for having been among the first in the world to give place and life to that basic human principle.

Meine sehr beliebte Freunde und Verwandten, vielen, vielen Dank! (Very dear friends and relatives: many, many thanks!)

CONCLUSION

If one listens well, one will hear in the voices of more and more of us, the voice of the Land Herself.

CHAPTER FOUR

THE *SIOUI* CASE EXPLAINED

"BRIDGES"

You may have all the locks and chains,
All the iron doors,
All the bulldozers
And all the dynamite,
But
You
Will always
Be
An
Outlaw
On my land,
You may hate me for speaking up,
You may dispossess, crush and
Discriminate me,
Try to starve me,
Post me up as "unwanted,"
Wish me to apologize for existing,
All you do here is illegal,
My land has not been in order
Since your disorder began.
You have no other decent, dignified choice
But to meet me halfway
On the bridges I have built

Before and since you came
And on others we need to build
Together.

The most valuable thing that can be transmitted to a child is faith
in nature, which is not merely love of nature but a guarantee
that such love can and will be lived out through actual personal
disposition and concrete action. Humans are born with a pure,
sovereign understanding that life is inclusive of all beings of all
orders; we arrive in this world possessing infinite awareness that
there is but one universal web of sacred relations uniting all life.
However, even before we are born the institutions that govern
our societies are already hard at work finding ways to sever that
formidable, ineffable power possessed by children from their
minds and souls. Pure, powerful circular thinkers are thus forever
targeted for quick and early transformation into linear thinkers.

That is how our societies, the world over, "produce the social
happiness of the majorities." The ultimate condition of that happiness is that "undue" sensitivity to nature must be done away with
so that everyone is able to think for the short term only. A child is
born able to think that the health of the Earth (Eatenonha) and of
all of us, Her children, must not be compromised, ever. After society
has done its work of desensitization, individuals, even young children, are able to go along with the vision of politicians and other
leaders about the health of the environment, of the Earth – a vision
that may not go beyond their present term in office. What then
passes for law, order, and progress is actually lawlessness, disorder,
and regression in those societies that, in actual fact, cannot be called
societies since this very word implies inclusion, togetherness, and
ability to see the circularity of life.

"Why are Aboriginal people generally resisting the order that
society imposes on them, on life as they conceive it to be?" I
always ask the students in my classes. "Is it only to cause trouble
to society, or simply because they don't have the mental wherewithal to understand how society has to be run?" Answering my
own question, I of course, say that it is because the whole logic of
their civilization tells them to resist, in the name of life itself and

of all that sustains it. Indigenous people resist in the name of all
the beings that are wantonly destroyed at every moment of every
day: the forests and their inhabitants, the water, the air, the rocks,
the people – especially the women, the children, the marginalized
in society, the homeless, the artists, other creators, and so many
people who have ended up in the jails for motives often invalid
and unjust.

In the course of "the great social brainwashing" that I have just
briefly described, most of us trade our inborn faith in nature for
faith in things produced and accomplished by humans. I remember that my grandmother Caroline knew a natural remedy for all
the common ills any one of us (her extended family that included
everyone, even passers-by who appeared and then disappeared
from among us) may be subject to. I remember a few times when
she proposed to give me one or another "almost natural" medicine that came from the store and that I would not take because
it was not "truly natural." This, of course, pleased her and she
would right away replace it with *un remède naturel*. Such an
anecdote is meant to illustrate how deeply our people insist on
ingraining in their offspring that faith in nature we have been
speaking about. I remember my mother giving me a few pieces of
gum she had just gotten from one of our tall, majestic spruce trees
standing close to our old log house and teaching me that we did
not need to buy chewing gum from the stores and, most interesting of all, that the gum which the trees gave us was healthy for
us, whereas the store-bought one was harmful to our teeth and
to our bodies.

"My dear relatives, my nieces and nephews," I used to tell my
students in my introductory classes (and at times in my more
advanced classes), "in a few years you are going to have children,
some of you already do. Our collective future depends on your
ability to infuse in them the faith in nature that has been and still
is the first and most important philosophical trait to be observed
in traditional Aboriginal cultures. It will be up to you to make
these children of yours able to converse closely, sentimentally, even
amorously with nature, with our common Mother, the Earth. If
we really want our children, our descendants, to be happy, secure,

and prosperous in an intelligent, viable way, we have to enable them to look at an animal, an insect, a flower, a tree, a sacred place that we feel has a special power, a mountain, a rivulet, an expression in the eyes of a living being, a cloud, a fish, an older person, another child, any manifestation of the life we universally share – we have to enable our children to look at all life, in all its expressions, and to speak with it in the universal language of our human souls. If we teach our children, our descendants, to truly look at nature as a Mother – the material manifestation of the infinite love of the Creator, the Great Spirit, the Great Mystery, God, Allah, Aronia,[1] Kitche Manito, Wakan Tanka, Krishna, any deity named by humans – they will possess that so essential, sacred faith in nature and they will themselves be enabled to transmit that faith to their own children and descendants.

"The fire of our humanity will be made strong again. We will then know we are able to not merely survive, we can be secure and happy and prosper all together. We can, at last, begin speaking the common language that has existed all along in our human souls, the language of mutual love, trust, understanding, and compassion. My dear relatives, my nephews and nieces, that is how I understand the teachings that my Elders, my people, have given to me to share with others, with you, with the world." (I have, of course, never used that exact wording in my classes; I am merely attempting to convey for you, my dear readers and friends, the sense of this teaching, which was always a central component in my classes.)

I ONCE WAS REBELLIOUS AND IGNORANT

Like many youth of my, or any, generation, I was once rebellious and ignorant. Not that I have today become a conformist and that I am much wiser; I have only become more conscious of my need to be a more constructive, more wholesome, more enlightened human being. Like every one of us, I struggle on that path every day and it is very rarely easy. But first, I wish to explain these two words, rebellious and ignorant, in the context of my personal evolution.

Rebellious. If you are an Indian, you were born a fighter. This, in the light of what we are discussing in this section dedicated to explaining the nature of the *Sioui* case, means that you are brought up to be a questioner, a disbeliever. To aptly illustrate this, I will use a quote taken from my book *For an Amerindian Autohistory*. In it, my father instructs me, his six-year-old first son, not to believe what is told to his History class. (This will further illustrate my father's thinking on education and the teaching of history; we have already touched upon this subject in the chapter "Seawi: Hurons of the Rising Sun".) What is also notable here is the care taken by my father to preserve in me, in his children, a sense of humanity and compassion for the ones who have invented that pernicious way of talking and thinking about our people's history. My father begins to pass on to me the duty of helping the newcomers and the world understand how we can reform the human bonds that have been damaged between us all, instead of merely and unproductively taking the stance of frustrated, manipulative victims: "My son, if you want to succeed in school and later on in life, you must write down what you are told to be the truth; but don't believe that it is the truth. Our ancestors were good and generous, and they lived very happily here, on their land. Our people have suffered a great deal since the white people came here, though it is not the white people's fault. The Great Spirit wants them to be here and He wants us to help them. One day you will write other books about history and help people to learn the truth. The day is coming when the Indians will be understood and cease to suffer. Time [as he often said] is the Father of Truth."

At that young age, my father sent me on a quest. (In fact, both my parents understood, in the same manner, their role regarding transmitting to their children a sense of our people's history.) However, as youth, we had to contend with the social realities as they materially existed around us: the ignorance, the indifference, the pervasive sense of being discriminated and rejected, therefore, the rebelliousness in me, in us, their children.

Ignorant. My father knew that in order to one day be able to write and help people learn about one's truth, enough knowledge must be acquired so that the writing has a chance of accomplishing its goal, at least in part. A tenet quite central in the education that I and my siblings received at home is that, as Hurons, the harshness of our historical trajectory has allowed us to retain only a partial, weakened sense of the original wisdom contained in our ancestral civilization. However, real hope to recover much of that original knowledge and strength of our people existed in our home thanks to our ability to see the close, powerful relationship that united all our Native nations.

I began to understand our common Aboriginal way of looking at life and at the world and to call it by its real name, that is, the circular way of thinking and seeing. I, and others of my generation, spent many years travelling to other Native communities for the mere sake of getting to know one another as the relatives that we are – living, talking, hunting, fishing, eating, smoking (as much as possible, pure Indian tobacco from the traditional Hodenosaunee people), drinking, and some of us experimenting with harmful drugs (though many of us promptly, almost "mysteriously," quit those pernicious habits soon after rediscovering our spiritual traditions through the teachings of our Elders). Mostly we were recreating ancestral bonds and forming new ones between us, some of those materializing in marriages (for example, six out of the seven of us siblings married and had children with Aboriginal persons of another Aboriginal nation).

We have also seen in a preceding section that the linkages that were eventually made with our sister-nations extend far and wide to comprise "the Four Americas," that is, Central and South America, including, of course, Brazil, the Portuguese-speaking America. This is because a leading principle in our familial education was that since there is strength in numbers and in unity, our network of alliances must encompass the whole continent of America.[2]

THE GENESIS OF THE *SIOUI* CASE

As mentioned at the beginning of this book and as recalled already, one of my principal aims is to impart to you, dear friend and reader, a new way of understanding our country's history so as to enable all of us to relate ever more profoundly, ever more trustingly, and

ever more affectionately to what our "country" truly is – our
Mother Earth. The following section will be about a legal battle
that was initiated and fought by my indomitable, non-conform-
ing family, the Siouis of the erstwhile Forty Arpents Reserve. The
whole episode lasted eight years and took us through four levels
of provincial and federal courts. We lost twice, the first time quite
badly, and eventually obtained a unanimous verdict in our Nation's
favour. It was, for our Nation and for all First Nations of Canada,
a landmark legal victory. As for our Huron-Wendat Nation, that
decision signified a renaissance at the cultural, economic, political,
and all other levels. Very importantly also, the Sioui decision has
served and continues to serve as a basis for the redefinition and the
reaffirmation of the Aboriginal Peoples' right to exist and evolve in
the modern world context.

In 1973, my mother founded the Amerindian Cultural Center
and the magazine *Kanatha,* of which I became the editor. Those
were very courageous creations; however, they always remained
quite fragile. Most of the five years that our magazine lived, we
barely managed to publish one or two editions a year. Eventually,
my own people encouraged me to apply to a job opening at the
Department of Indian Affairs, in Ottawa. The position was officer
of literature and communications and comprised the editorship of
the then renowned Indian cultural magazine *Tawow.* I had been
wholly committed to *Kanatha* and would never have left it if my
own relatives (including, of course, my mother) and closest friends
had not made me see the sheer impossibility of accomplishing the
lofty goals we had for *Kanatha* within the constricted, stifling, colonized confines of the Reserve. I got the position and when I went
to Ottawa, I found the world waiting for me!

In Ottawa, mostly because of my functions as editor, I got to
know and become friends with many prominent Aboriginal artists and thinkers. Most importantly, I got to meet Elders, especially from the Western provinces where, as I found out, many
of our Native spiritual traditions were, and still are, better preserved than in most of our eastern communities. To go straight
to the subject of this present section, which is the explanation
of the *Sioui* case, I and some of my friends eventually met Cree,

Saulteaux, and Nakoda Elders from Alberta who, in the spring of 1980, invited us to their territory to do a traditional fast and to participate in some ceremonies. I will now explain how and why the famed *Sioui* case had its genesis in Alberta, in a traditional spiritual location in the territory of the Nakoda people, and not in the Province of Quebec as is still thought in many political circles in my own Nation and elsewhere. If one should ask most of the concerned people or even the jurists who worked on the *Sioui* case how the case originated or how was it won, you would likely get this approximate answer: There were these guys, the Sioui brothers, who were in a serious legal bind. They had taken serious chances with the rights of our Nation, which, fortunately for these individuals, was able and willing to lend them important documents with which some of their very skilful lawyers were (almost miraculously) successful in winning this case for the Huron-Wendat Nation, thereby allowing these four wayward individuals to come out free in the end.

THE CASE

The reason I have given some personal and family details in this section is that I have been the protagonist of the case.[3] As already alluded to, the greatest enrichment to my new life in Ottawa was meeting Indian Elders from the Canadian Prairies. As I also mentioned before, the *Sioui* case had its origin in Alberta, the sacred territory of the Nakoda (or Stoney or Assiniboine) Nation. That territory is referred to in English as the Kootenay Plains. At the insistence of my late Ojibway friend Herb Nabigon, who had previously been in that location and had begun to be taught by these same Elders, I and another friend, the late renowned Ojibway painter Roy Thomas,[4] decided to accept the invitation extended to the three of us. The three Elders, all widely respected Medicine Men, now all deceased, were Peter Ochiese, a very famous Saulteaux spiritualist who left us in 2006 at 114 years old; Abraham Burnstick, a Cree-Nakoda Elder; and Eddy Bellerose, a Cree spiritualist and philosopher. All three are fondly remembered by many as persons of great wisdom and love who, until the very end of their lives, used their knowledge to help and heal people of all origins. These were people whose presence in my life would be quite determining in my own quest for knowledge and wisdom and who, pointedly, were the actual primary founders of the *Sioui* case.

It was May 1982. This was going to be our third consecutive annual spiritual fast together, Roy, Herb, and I. The first had been on the Kootenay Plains, in Alberta. Among us were also two women friends, Alice and Bernadette, not girlfriends, just good women friends. Also being instructed on Native spirituality were seven Catholic priests who, of course, became everyone else's friends. We all had a wonderful, magical time, knowing we were getting (re-)acquainted with the ancestral spiritual traditions of Amerindian peoples and, in our own case as Native persons, with intimate, sacred aspects of our own Aboriginal civilization. We had a great feeling of joy because we knew we were being led on a path of very important self-fulfillment, as (up until then) rebellious, ignorant, deeply colonized young Aboriginal individuals.

Herb, Roy, and I did our second fast just the three of us together in a quiet, wooded part not very far from Ottawa, on top of one of the highest hills in the vicinity. After our first such experience the year before, our shared feeling was that we had to start helping spread this sort of knowledge and awareness back out east, where decades, even centuries of colonial repression had had the sad result of making most of our Indian, Métis, and Inuit peoples abandon and/or forget their traditional spiritual ways. They had become the poorest and most marginalized people in the land they had such obvious entitlement to call their own, their Eatenonha, their Mother Earth. Our second fast (they are all of four days without food and water) went very well and we felt quite proud and honoured to have taken on the task, in a very small simple way, of helping with the healing of our people, of all people. As all our Elders say, it is our ultimate responsibility as the First Peoples of this land to help instill in all Her human children the kind of faith, humility, and love that leads to an understanding of why and how we will better ensure the happiness and the security of all of our descendants, in the seventh generation hence and beyond.

In May 1982, Roy Thomas had some urgent business to attend to in his artist's life, so Herb and I prepared for our fast and went alone. For that year, I had suggested to my two friends that we conduct our fast in my people's traditional territory, in the Province of Quebec. I had also informed my friends that, having no recognized territorial rights of our own anywhere except in our tiny Reserve, we were likely to be disturbed during our fast and even be ordered out of the park by the conservation officers (*agents de la conservation*) of the Ministry of Forests, Wildlife, and Parks. It will be noted here that the Parc des Laurentides had been created in 1904 by the Government of Quebec from territories traditionally occupied by the Huron-Wendat and the Innu Nations, without any form of consultation with either Nation. Our people had simply been told not to go back to their ancestral hunting grounds or risk constant harassment while trying to earn their living in the woods, harsh penalties in the form of fines, or, much more likely since we were all poor, prison.

Members of a few Huron-Wendat former Forty Arpents families and a few others had, however, continued to be instructed by their Elders that those forests were still ours by customary law, that we were simply intimidated by the government to leave them, and that we, the younger people, should keep affirming our ancestral right through our continued physical occupation of those territories. "Using force does not produce a right; using force to gain a right is a crime," our Elders reminded us when speaking of the ways we, as a people, had been and continued to be robbed and denied our "right to be" (as my mother used to say). In my youth, it was no longer possible for the non-Native society to "get rid of" Indians and get away with it, so we became even bolder than our predecessors. Many times, in the 1970s and early 1980s, we met, in those home forests of ours, conservation officers who gave us fines to pay. Determined to one day take that government to court in order to bring to examination the question of our rights in that park, we told those agents every time that we were not going to pay those fines and that we sought to go to court with their Ministry. In response, we would typically be asked: "Why are you, the Siouis, so hard-headed? All the other

Hurons are able to recognize when they have contravened with the law and they pay their fines." "We are not concerned with what other Hurons do about their fines," was our usual answer. "We are only seeking to determine, with your society, what our rights are on these territories that we believe are still ours. We also want to find out, with everyone's help, how we can better protect these lands, all together." We then saw the same scenario every time these encounters occurred; the agents went to their vehicles and called their superiors in Quebec City. Every time, the officers came back to us showing some shyness and used a friendly tone to tell us that their bosses instructed them to let us go. We would then, at times, exchange a few expressions of hope of one day finding some way of redressing wrongs of the past so as to live more contentedly all together, Québécois and Native people. This kind of "circular approach" to our quest for recognition was going to be the hallmark of the Sioui decision and what made us, in the name of our whole nation, and truly of the whole society, victorious in the end.

The greatest gift we received from our Western Elders and relatives was a sense of sovereign assurance that our own Aboriginal civilization possessed the answers to every deep question we harboured about our identity and our history as young Native persons. Their love and their wisdom produced a rapid, deep transformation not just in some of us, but in all of us who had the invaluable chance to know them and learn from them.

It was nothing short of magical, all we needed in order to leave our rebellious and resentful beings behind and become proud of ourselves, and kind and compassionate toward anyone else, was to be touched by them in our hearts and spirits. The Sioui case was born then and there: we would be enabled to present ourselves to the several successive courts (right up to the Supreme Court of Canada) in the non-confrontational, non-threatening manner of the "old Indian way," in the Way of the Circle. We would not be claiming millions and millions of dollars, we only wanted the freedom to practice our ancestral customs and rediscover the deeper sense of our identity. We were determined to have a certain document, dated 5 September 1760, which our Nation held in its archives, recognized as a Treaty made between us and the British Crown. The aim was for all parties to that Treaty to gain something important: the desire and the knowledge of how to recognize one another and of how to relate together, after a long time of ignoring how to do so and, therefore, of not living well together. I will now explain how an old, "dead" document received a new life by being looked at in the light of our ancestral spiritual tradition and thus produced an unlikely victory in Canada's highest court.

THE DOCUMENT

The document, now a recognized Treaty, was drafted on the battlefield and signed by British commander James Murray. It reads as follows:

> These are to certify that the Chief of the Huron Tribe of Indians, having come to me in the name of His Nation to submit to His Britannick Majesty, and make Peace, has been received under my Protection, with his whole Tribe; and henceforth no English Officer or party is to molest, or interrupt them in returning to their Settlement at Lorette; and they are received upon the same terms with the Canadians, being allowed the free Exercise of their Religion, their Customs, and Liberty of trading with the English: recommending it to the officers commanding the posts to treat them kindly.
>
> James A. Murray
> Commander-in-Chief
> September 5th, 1760

To be sure, this document, upon and after its creation in 1760, was seen by our people as a very precious possession since it guaranteed, under the new regime of the victorious British, the protection and the continuation of everything that made up our identity in terms of our material culture and our spiritual traditions. However, our Headmen, Elders, and Clan Mothers, in the defence of their rights, produced their Treaty in many successive political and legal arenas all along the decades that followed, but

to no avail. The authorities of Lower Canada (part of this territorial entity eventually became the Province of Quebec) called
our Treaty a mere "safe conduct," that is, a document given to
our people at the end of the hostilities (the Seven Years War) to
enable them to return to their homes without being molested or
attacked by the English soldiers and garrisons. Over time, our
Treaty became a dead, albeit interesting, piece of archival material forgotten by all but a very few individuals in our Nation, such
as my late dear friend and fellow historian François Vincent, col-
lector and keeper of that and many more very important objects
and papers that are part of our ancestors' legacy.

As previously mentioned, it had been my initiative to arrange
and plan for our third spiritual fast in my Nation's traditional
territory (in many of my people's eyes, illegally appropriated by
the Province of Quebec). At this point, dear reader, I wish to recall
the fundamental goal I am pursuing in the present essay by making the following assertion: it would not be possible to approach
a case such as this one from a linear, patriarchal perspective and
build it so as to obtain a victory, especially one as resounding as
the one we obtained in Canada's Supreme Court. The only way to
understand this victory of our Nation is to look at this case from
a circular and matricentric, that is, Indigenous vantage point.

I and my Neechee (Friend and Brother) Herb Nabigon had
made our sleeping lodges out of willow saplings, cut ceremonially
using tobacco as an offering in recognition of the gift from our
Mother Earth.[5] We had also made a simple fireplace to warm
ourselves at night. These two facts served as the basis for the two
"infractions" we were charged with. Our case was first heard in
the spring of 1983, one year after the events that led to the accu-
sations. In June, we were summarily condemned in the Cour des
Sessions de la Paix and ordered to pay our fines.

Three of my brothers were also involved in the case – Régent,
Konrad, and Hugues, along with their families, were camped
about one kilometre away from our place of fasting. All their
children were still small then and this, for these young families, was another fun trip to the forest, a merry adventure in an
enchanted world that was the domain of the trout, partridges,

hares, moose, bears, and so many other wonderful, beautiful peoples of our woods. Éléonore, the grandmother, was also there getting the children acquainted with many plant-relatives, infusing in the children that so precious faith and love of Nature, our ultimate Mother, our Eatenonha – a feeling and a knowledge that more than anything else makes us who we are and that would colour throughout their lives every important thought and action of these children, these future fathers and mothers of our Nation.

I was, among us (the four involved Sioui brothers), the one principally inculpated in the court case.[6] Since it revolved around a spiritualist approach to our defence and since the life path I had been on for a few years had led me to undertake this legal action, I chose not to be assisted by a lawyer. I was convinced (and of course, still am) that no lawyer in the country at that time had the expertise and the knowledge for explaining in any court of law the philosophical and cultural concepts I wished to see our case based on. My three brothers, as to themselves, chose to be represented by an attorney. My own testimonies in the initial stages of the legal process have provided the logic and have become the spirit of the case. Since I was trained and instructed by many Elders and teachers along my path, it was my responsibility to fulfill that role, and I am both proud and thankful that I was able to serve in this manner. My task, as I understood it, was to bring and keep the whole matter into Indigenous philosophical territory by steering away from the linear, confrontational approach to Indigenous claims – territorial, cultural, or otherwise.

As the leader in this case, my goal was to impress on the successive courts of justice we would have to face that our Huron and Native tradition prescribed that the whole society that we formed all together was a circle and that a circle has no sides, which means that we all had to come out winners. As Dakota (Sioux) Headman Tatanka Iyotake (Sitting Bull) once said in a Council with non-Native authorities: "Let us put our minds together and see what future we can create for our children." This approach to our struggle, which I have been speaking of as the secret to our victory in the Supreme Court, was what readily won us the help and the support of not only a great number of Aboriginal social, cultural, and political organizations and individuals in the country and internationally, but also and most importantly, of a whole host of non-Aboriginal organizations of every sort. The momentum quickly became strong and very wide because everyone, of every ethnic and cultural background, could see what was in it for him/her, for her/his group, and for the world collectivity.

Why do I and others always refer to this sort of thinking as matricentric or, without using this new terminology, inevitably get to speak about the central importance of women (traditionally, all women and those who identify as women are mothers of the nation) and about the central place that women still occupy in traditional Native societies? This respect and honour given to women and to womanhood is probably the most constant cultural trait that one can note in the words and in the behaviour of traditional Indigenous persons. "We all come to this world carried in our mother's womb," we often hear wise people say. Women know much more intimately than men the value of their offspring's life; women are the first creators and, therefore, the beings ordained by Nature as the nurturers of human societies, and the same goes for other-than-human peoples. This special sensitivity and attentiveness to life, which is a woman's inborn attribute, is what is implied in the expression "circular thinking." It implies the notion that I have proposed before that it is not possible for a patriarchal/patricentric society to impart to its members the kind of social sensitivity that is able to engender real social potential for long-term survival. It also implies, as I have also suggested before in this essay, that patriarchal societies – almost all human societies have evolved from matricentric to patricentric over time – cannot properly be called societies. In virtual absence of sufficient attentiveness and reverence for life and its living sources, patriarchal societies depend for their survival on the mere physical exploitation and the wasting of Earth's natural resources, that is, Eatenonha's body and lifeblood. That is how and why my relatives and I saw and continue to see our struggle, which has come to be referred to as the *Sioui* case. The *Sioui* case has countless other equivalents the world over, mainly among the Indigenous world. That is why the *Sioui* case is ongoing and will never end: it is much too important and besides, it is gaining new adherents every day.

When the conservation officers came to evict us from the park, on our third day of fasting, my mother Éléonore (today, 20 May, is the day of her birth), in a very tranquil though determined mood, explained to these two men that our quest as a family representing our and all other Native nations in America, was to offer the non-Indigenous society new ideas and ways of caring about Nature. She remarked that the use of the word *conservation* to designate the vocation of that park (Parc de la Conservation) was not appropriate since large parts of those forests had already been clear-cut. Of course, we did comply with the agents' order to leave ("or else a police detachment would be coming the day after to take us out forcibly"). Before parting company, we came to amiable terms together and, again, our Clan Mother Éléonore informed the officers that this was the beginning of a long, laborious legal process and that, following our traditional Huron way of thinking, a true victory would mean that we would all (Quebecers and all of us together) find in an eventual legal decision our fair share of advantages, as well as responsibilities. The officers wished us good luck and we shook hands with them.

EPILOGUE

Eight years after almost to the day, on 29 May 1990, after a seemingly endless battle that took us through four different courts of law and that, as we now know, was won, we came back to our fasting place, abandoned (temporarily) in May 1982. We removed the green moss that had grown on "our" stones and we re-lit our fire and made a simple Thanksgiving Ceremony. Some conservation officers happened to come around. They were new ones but knew very well about our case and about our very recent victory. They came out of their vehicles, with polite, shy smiles on their faces, and congratulated us. We had a brief, friendly talk and they left. It was a beautiful, magical day – a day to be very especially thankful for. In the good, joyful warmth of that day in late May, with patches of snow still laying on the forest floor and with majestic

Lake Sotoriski down below, still asleep under its blanket of ice, I remember thinking and saying that this was the first time in my life I felt I could think of myself as a Canadian. Indeed, Canada had shown me, had shown us, Seawi, Wendat, Indians, all Canadians, that she was able to live by the idea that before being a nation-state, she understands and is able to live by the idea that she is her children's Mother Earth, their, *our* Eatenonha. I am and forever will be a Wendat first. However, that day of our Supreme Court victory, I understood that being Wendat meant being very deeply Canadian and, therefore, responsible for helping to impart to my fellow countrypeople that same way of feeling and being.[7]

CHAPTER FIVE

THE ESSENTIAL THREAD OF CANADA'S HISTORY

"LIVING HISTORY"

Those who live on the edge
Of survival
Are the very heart
Of history
I am a Wendat
I am the living History

This section of my essay will bring full meaning to the intent expressed in the first paragraph of this book, that of making the gift to my fellow Canadians and to the world of a deeper, "Indigenized" sense of our common history. Thus far, I have illustrated through personal and family histories how knowledge of an essential sense of our own history and, therefore, of Canadian history, has been kept alive in my people, especially in my Seawi Clan. One thing that will have become evident is that I, among my family and people, have inherited the special role of guardian and interpreter of our history. I wish at this moment to illustrate the extent to which I have actualized my people's expectations toward me and how I have come to look at my life in relation to this role. I am using two entries from my personal diary.

I am a highly important person. I am, I believe, the only human being able to reveal and explain the true thread

of the history of this country, of this continent, of our
Indigenous world. (On a train from Edmonton to Jasper,
Alberta, 7 July 2007)

A good, healthy understanding of Canada's history will be the
guarantee of a strong and healthy Canada. That is what I am
able to offer, more perhaps than any other past, present, or
future historian. (Ottawa, 17 June 2011)

THE PLACE AND ROLE OF THE WENDAT
IN ABORIGINAL GEOPOLITICS

As a Wendat, mindful of the instructions received early in life
from my parents and community and in my professional role as
teacher and educator over the past four decades, it has been my
untiring quest to denounce and refute the many negative notions
entertained by the larger society about us, Aboriginal Peoples.
Such social anti-Indian mythology has allowed our country, just
as has happened in all colonial nation-states, to keep us marginalized and to continue to dispossess us, as well as maintain among
our newly-come relatives an optimal level of insensitivity toward
us, the Aboriginal Peoples and, by way of consequence, with (out)
regard to our common Earth Mother, our Eatenonha.

The next several pages will expose some of the argumentation
that I have developed (some of it, of course, inspired by others) and
used to attempt to reach my goals. Firstly, I will share with you,
dear reader and relative, a brief introduction to a course I created
in 2007 as a graduate-level seminar, and that I have given, in an
adapted form, as a fourth-year BA class every year afterwards, alter-
nately in French and in English. The title of my course was, until
my retirement in December 2016, Nadowek and Algonquians:
Canada's First Civilization.

First, an explanation of the term *Nadowek*. The word *Nadowek*,
an Algonquian term meaning "people of a different stock," aims to
replace the common term *Iroquoian*, which is customarily used to
designate the linguistic family that originally comprised the Five
"Iroquois" Nations (whose actual autonym is Hodenosaunee, that

is, People of the Longhouse). It also includes the other erstwhile "Iroquoian" Confederacies: the Erie, or People of the Cougar; the Attiwandaronk, or Neutral; the Tionontate, or People of the Hills, also named the Tobacco, or Petun (an old French word for tobacco, itself borrowed from an Indigenous language of Brazil); the Stadacona; the Hochelaga; the Susquehanna, or Conestoga; the Tuscarora; and the Cherokee. Other entities, or Nations, such as the Meherrin and the Wenro, who disappeared early after contact with the Europeans and whose remnants survived, as was the case for all other remnants of dispersed Native peoples, by merging with other Confederacies and Nations, mostly of their own Nadowek stock in this case, but also of the Algonquian linguistic family (the most numerous and territorially extended family of nations in the region of the Northeast) are included as well. The other three linguistic families present in the Northeast were the Siouan (Dakota, Nakoda, Lakota, Winnebago, and many others); the Beothuk, the original inhabitants of the Island of Newfoundland; and the Inuit, the People of the Far North.

By replacing the term *Iroquoian* with *Nadowek*, I also intend to recall the original geopolitical situation established by the Aboriginal Peoples on their continent long before any European adventurers began to form the project of "discovering" new "pagan" lands for their sovereigns and churches. As we shall see presently, the term *Iroquoian* has had the unfortunate (though convenient for the colonial authorities) consequence of making of the Hodenosaunee ("the Iroquois") the paramount example of savagery and inadequacy as humans that the good, God-fearing, valiant settlers had the noble mission of annihilating completely. The "Iroquois," who, as their entire history so patently and eloquently demonstrates, fully deserve the reputation of courage and intelligence that they have secured for themselves as a People, did not originally have the political centrality that European and non-Native historians and writers have made them out to have.

By changing this terminology, I wish to also suggest that, as oral traditions, archaeology, and linguistics concur to demonstrate, the Nadowek arrived in the Northeast later than the Algonquians who were the first to migrate north in remote times after the glaciers melted. It is for this reason that we – the Nadowek – should be named collectively by a name that many Algonquians called us by ("People of Another Stock"). Finally, what I also aim at through this change of names is to see my Hodenosaunee kinfolk relieved of the immense, oppressive, unjust, and undeserved historical burden laid on them through the terminological contraptions that the names "Iroquois" and "Iroquoians" truly are. Now, to define what I term "Canada's first civilization," I am using an extract from my course syllabus:

The Nadowek-Algonquian civilization is the Aboriginal civilization that began to be elaborated before AD 1000 on the territory that witnessed Canada's birth in the sixteenth and seventeenth centuries. Our class will be an exercise in the study of the pre-European origins of modern-day Canada. Our main task will be to research the historical and philosophical continuum existing between, on the one hand, the social ideals which gave rise to the Nadowek-Algonquian civilization and, on the other hand, the social ideals which underlie the character of Canada as we know it. Other American nation-states, such as Mexico, the United States, Bolivia, Ecuador, and Peru, have reflected more than we Canadians have about their Aboriginal socio-political heritage. For example, a number of political theorists have argued that the United States have conceived their own constitutional notions, as well as their particular expansionist mission from the model that, with some reason, they purport to have learned from the Hodenosaunee (the League of the Five Iroquois Nations). How does our own Canadian Aboriginal socio-political heritage, especially the one originating from the civilization that we are to study, make us a different people, a different society? What are the main reasons why this fundamental aspect of the history of Canada has been evacuated from the official discourse on Canadian history and what are the societal consequences of such evacuation?

What is, for Canada, the heritage of the Nadowek (Wendat, Erie, Stadacona, Hodenosaunee, Neutral, and others) and of the Algonquian (Odawa, Nipissing, Mississauga, Cree, Attikamek, Anishinabek, Mi'kmaq and others) who, originally, partook in and are still heirs to the Nadowek-Algonquian civilization? We shall, in this class, explore this largely unrecognized founding Canadian civilization, and the circumstances in which many of these participating peoples and nations ceased to exist as human and social entities, as well as the interest of the knowledge of the history of this civilization for an increased understanding of the deeper nature of our country, Canada. We shall also research ways of creating new methodologies for the study of the history and the sociology of Aboriginal/Indigenous peoples, generally.

Starting from their own scholarly interest based on written sources and/or the Aboriginal oral traditions, class members will choose an area of research, such as political ideas, culture and spirituality, subsistence and ecology, commerce and economy, gender relations, international relations, education, artistic expression, etc., and help create new knowledge about the history, philosophy, and sociology of the Aboriginal Peoples of Canada and elsewhere.

This is again the moment to remind ourselves, dear reader, of the fundamental goal that I am pursuing in this essay. As we have seen on several occasions, that goal is to help us deepen our sense of rootedness in the soil where we make our home, that is, Canada. We are now, in this section, embarking on a very crucial part of an effort to learn how the peoples native to this land have thought out, over the millennia, how to organize their existence in the best possible ways, that is, by being attentive to the feelings, the moods, the ideas, the language of their Earth Mother, their Eatenonha. What we are, in fact, attempting to achieve for ourselves when revisiting the foundations of our country's colonial historiography, using an Aboriginal perspective, is to enable ourselves to learn, for the immediate and the more distant future, how to build our society in ways that take inspiration from models inherited from the first civilization(s) of Canada.

At the very heart of this vast collective enterprise of discovery of such models is the question that we have been contemplating throughout this essay: How do we increase in our citizenry the capacity for sensitivity toward the natural world, the environment, Mother Earth, our Eatenonha? This, of course, begs the question: Why and how are we to empower women to regain their central place in a human community? And, why and how must we encourage and inspire men to leave that central place to women and to realize the utter danger for all of us, the whole Circle of Life, of continuing with this disorder that has been and continues to be the source of so much confusion all around us? And then, very pointedly, the question of leadership: What makes a leader in a society where a circular approach to life is cultivated? How are leaders identified, raised, and appointed in a circular-thinking society, as compared to what happens in a linear-thinking one, that is, on either side of the civilizational divide (to, one day, do away with this divide)? We shall see further on how these differences in the realm of socio-political ideas have very determining incidences on almost every other aspect of social living and institution building.

Now, let us take a direct look at two of the questions that were posed in that syllabus: How does our own Canadian socio-political heritage, especially the one originating from the civilization that we are to study, make us a different people, a different society? What are the main reasons why this fundamental aspect of the history of Canada has been evacuated from the official discourse on Canadian history and what are the societal consequences of such evacuation? I see two evident reasons needing to be stated here: first, the need for the (linear-thinking) colonizers to appropriate the territory; and second, hinging on the first, the need for the colonial elites to instill in the citizenry of "their" new country the notion that the ones thus dispossessed did not know what to do with that territory and, therefore, did not deserve to occupy, let alone "own" it. There is more knowledge now, among the newer generations that the notion of owning the land does not concord with the circular way of thinking of the Indigenous peoples; rather, one belongs to the Earth, as one belongs to one's mother and father, one's family.

In the case of the Nadowek-Algonquian civilization, one so central to Canada's formation as a new country, it was of first importance for the original writers of Canada's history to paint an especially dreadful picture of what the Aboriginal geopolitical arrangement vested in that civilization consisted of. Basically, a sophisticated, ideologically and morally refined society of Native nations which could and should have provided an unassailable basis for the future internal pride and global respectability of a country such as Canada was, in the official books of our history, made out to look like the epitome of human social dysfunctionality and irrationality. The sad result is that this mythology has been internalized by a very large part of the Canadian population and is still presented as truth in the majority of textbooks available in the Canadian school system.

I have chosen to reproduce here three texts that I have already published, the first two in my *Histories of Kanatha*[1] and the third in my *Huron-Wendat: The Heritage of the Circle*. I consider these texts quintessential for exposing the "myth of the victorious Iroquois," a historiographical forgery that I have described as "the cornerstone of conventional Canadian history" in my first book, *For an Amerindian Autohistory*. The end goal pursued in joining these three texts is to enable my reader (and the Canadian public) to understand the original configuration of an Aboriginal geopolitical order, long established at the time of the European arrival, and thus to capture the sense of how the history of what was to be Canada predated the time our peoples and their land came into contact with Europeans. Again, my goal is to offer to my reader, to all Canadians, and to the world, an insight into why Canada is such a special place and why and how it can be even more admired and revered. This Aboriginal narrative has for very long been buried under a gigantic heap of very well-crafted falsehoods that get repeated whenever we, Canadians, venture to speak about the beginnings of our country.

First, a poem:

"UNWRITE INDIAN HISTORY"
(To my black relatives, especially to Corky McClerkin, my late brother and a truly great jazz pianist of Chicago.)

Fortunate are our Black relatives
Who have a History
That no one can distort

Black and white and mindlessly cruel
For anyone to read,
Testify and observe
Pity my Red people,
Who remember though they should not,
Because someone else took the pen
And wrote our History
After the end of our world
Was deemed accomplished.

Make the Indian a part
Of your great democracy,
Give him your justice,
"Rewrite" his History,
Grant him your self-government,
Extend to him your education,
Tell him even that you accept
His beautiful, wonderful cultures
As part of your great New World legacy
Include them all,
Except the ones who remember and speak,
And write, sing, carve, paint or dance
With their blood, with their soul.
Do not remember
Even though you do!
For Indian amnesia
Is a central pillar
Of our great democracy.

Sometimes, I wish I could trade our History
for that of my Black brothers and sisters
And just play music and dance together
And just quit bothering about History.

The first text:

Coming now to what I have termed the cornerstone of
non-Native Canadian historiography, that is, the "destruction

of the Hurons by the Iroquois," descriptions by early
European historians (essentially French Jesuits) show the
people of these two Confederacies (the Wendat and the
Hodenosaunee) living by exactly the same moral and social
ideals. They acknowledged the perfection of an all-power-
ful Creation, the interdependence of all beings, the inherent
vulnerability of the human and his/her essential duty to share
with others whatever wealth he/she is fortunate enough to
obtain. Historical records are eloquent about the astonish-
ing capacity of these two peoples to create peace between
themselves in spite of constant, systematic, and sometimes
concerted efforts of theoretically rival European powers.
Archaeology shows no conclusive proofs of the existence
of seriously destructive or prolonged prehistoric conflicts
between them. In fact, the early historical record, as well as
oral tradition and archaeology itself, all amply indicate that
the so-called wars that many Wendat-Iroquoian (or Nadowek,
as they were called by their Algonquian neighbours) people
waged on one another were mere "mourning wars." These
were normally organized – or countered – by Councils of
Ancients and Councils of Clanmothers to effect the capture
of a few enemies destined either to replace some male or
female member of the family, Clan, Nation or Confederacy
lost through war or some other cause, or to die by torture and
fire if the offence suffered by the people concerned demanded
such satisfaction. It should be noted that such executions were
performed in a communal way, and that the captives lived out
their ordeal until death with the most exemplary calmness
and fortitude. Such "wars" carried no notion of a need to
exterminate other human entities for profit and consequently
should not be put (as they commonly are) on a cultural par
with what Europeans, Euro-Americans, and others meant and
still mean by war.

A central fact in the social ethics of Western civilization is
that war is almost the only way to win something. This cultural
trait is necessarily and universally projected upon the "con-
quered" people, thus justifying the global war process on which
that civilization thrives. This same logic was applied to the

historiography of the Hodenosaunee. However, historical documents and the Iroquois oral traditions, as well as the memory stored and kept in wampums, masks, condolence canes,
and other sacred word-enshrining ceremonies and objects, all
speak profusely and eloquently about the Hodenosaunee's
social and spiritual vision. Written and oral sources, especially the Hodenosaunee's own, show that this Aboriginal
Confederacy had done an imposing amount of practical
thinking on how peace could be possessed and extended to
the rest of the universe.

During the first decades after contact, the destruction
by epidemic diseases of the great majority of the original
human population of the American hemisphere, though so
thoroughly documented in the primary sources, was hardly
mentioned by the first historiographers who took on the task
of producing the histories of the newly formed New World
states. Instead, it was deemed quite convenient to place the
blame for the human destruction on certain Native nations or
groups of nations. The Iroquois were among the ones granted
the privilege of that role. From being a group of Aboriginal
nations which, by the time of European arrival, had achieved
a high degree of political stability inside and around their own
world, the Hodenosaunee passed to being, in the accounts
of the invaders, an essentially irrational set of human beings,
intent on destroying anyone they came near to, an utter mistake of the Creator that could only be amended through extir-
pation. During almost the whole seventeenth century, France
conceived a central part of its moral and political duty in New
France to be precisely this: the extermination of the Iroquois.

What were the original Hodenosaunee in the geopolitical
reality? In the Amerindian world in the Northeast, their geopolitical situation was marginal. At the moment of contact,
the Five Iroquois Nations appeared to be dissenting from
the general trading system in use among the vast majority of
Native nations with which they were in contact. That system
– at the centre of which were the Wendat, whose language
was universally used in trade and diplomacy – included

virtually all the other Algonquian and Nadowek Nations of the vast region of the Northeast, surrounding, in fact, the Hodenosaunee on all sides.

Why did the Iroquois appear dissenting at that moment? My conjecture is that some political stress, probably related to the appearance of the deadly Old World diseases, came at a very early moment after contact (prominent demographer Henry F. Dobyns has surmised around 1524), and upset the existing balance of forces. At any rate, no explanation given so far has proven satisfactory in terms of all the existing evidence. Although old racist and deterministic theories have now been discredited, none of the newer ones has been able to offset the stereotype of the "Imperial Iroquois." Francis Jennings, in his landmark book *The Ambiguous Iroquois Empire*, while efficiently denouncing the myth of an "Iroquois empire" in the 17th and 18th centuries, does not basically alter the negative image affecting the Iroquois. They are still easily imagined as hailing the arrival of the white man on the political scene of the Northeast as a means of procuring the wherewithal to bring down their enemies and establish themselves at the centre of a thus-emptied Amerindian world and of a new colonial political game where they would wield lots of power.

The pathetic reality is that because they were not in the Wendat country – or Wendake – the Hodenosaunee, though also very severely affected by the European epidemics, did not have to face the European enemy directly. This meant that the Hodenosaunee was not compelled to abide by all the conditions of trade imposed on the Wendat-Algonquian alliance, the direst of which was the religious condition, which imposed the presence of several missionaries in each of the principal Wendat towns. Obviously, the Black Robes, besides being prime spiritual and social destabilizers, were real though unwitting biological warmongers. Under the cataclysmic circumstances that, according to the Jesuit Relations, then prevailed throughout the Amerindian country, the Hodenosaunee acted out the role that they knew was theirs – they gathered, *manu militari*, the remnants of rapidly disappearing Native nations around them. According to Wendat-Hodenosaunee social practice, defeated peoples were formally adopted and made room for as equals and, indeed, relatives. The present-day Iroquois are, in fact, descendants of an amalgam of refugees and adoptees from several dozens of Native nations. Their heritage even includes European adoptees who, as a rule, elected to remain Iroquois when offered the opportunity to return to their own people, a fact that demonstrates the more humane nature of Amerindian concepts of race and identity compared to Euro-American ones.

By combining the Hodenosaunee's perception of their own particular social ethics with the widest possible range of historical evidence, the *autohistorical method* makes the Hodenosaunee appear not as a race of senseless butchers lusting after European trade goods, guns, and power, but rather as people desperately trying to find an alternative to the French, Dutch, and English "Indian policies" that were reducing and engulfing all Amerindians. This is no slight conceptual turnabout. It presents the possibility of untangling one of the most masterful historiographical manipulations effected by the original historians of the invading Europeans.

The re-reading of the Wendat-Hodenosaunee history of contact offers hope for a cure for the old "Iroquois-destroyed-Huron" paradigm, which has been an important part of the moral and spiritual burden felt and carried by all Amerindians in relation to our collective "post-contact" history.

The second text was published in the Acts of an international conference of anthropology held in Quebec City in November 2007: "Anthropologie des cultures globalisées. Terrains complexes et enjeux disciplinaires."[2] The following is an excerpt from my presentation "Les premières civilisations des Amériques. Retour sur l'histoire dans l'anthropologie," originally given in French and which I am translating here to English. I have chosen to include it in the present essay as it pointedly addresses the task I have defined for the present section, that of capturing and exposing the original thread of our country's history, as kept and preserved in my Nation, Clan, and family.

The second text:

The most common feeling defining the perception that Aboriginal (and many non-Aboriginal) Canadians have had and still have about history is that it is a "set of lies," *un paquet de menteries*, as goes the real Québécois expression. To be sure, Canada is not the only country where folks in general live and die feeling helplessly that "someone" (meaning society, or "the system") has not wanted that the "real history" be known. Quite simply, there is in the air of our country, as in that of many others, the feeling that one must believe, even while knowing it is not true, in the history one is told about our nation's origins, and love that history, even venerate it, somewhat like we had to with religion at the time not so remote when it was socially recommended to mistreat the unbeliever.

As a starting point for this part of my remarks, I have chosen to expose and discuss a myth quite unacknowledged relating to our Canadian and Québécois history and that I deem very central to it: the myth of the victorious Iroquois. "So," some will say, "here is one Huron who, three and a half centuries after the events, still has not admitted his people's defeat by the Iroquois." In *For an Amerindian Autohistory*, I have already spoken of the so-called destruction of the Huron by the Iroquois as "the cornerstone of the traditional Amerindian heterohistory in the Northeast." While I do not desire to modify what I have written on that subject, I wish to explain today why I think it is vital for the sound evolution of the magnificent, promising country that Canada is to carefully examine this notion, which my own people perceive as one of those lies of history. I envision that in choosing to utilize this unsuspected historiographical key we, as a country, will accede to a liberating, proud, and unifying vision of our common history.

First, it is necessary to go back in time to the beginning of the thirteenth century of our era. We can see from modern archaeological evidence and the extant oral tradition, that the

ancestors of the Wendat, already possessing rich, secular commercial and diplomatic relations uniting them to a great many
peoples belonging to four distinct linguistic families (namely,
Nadowek (or Iroquoian), Algonquian, Siouan, and Beothuk)
undertook to create Wendake (pronounced Won-da-keh), an
international agricultural and commercial heartland situated
between present-day lakes Huron and Simcoe (less than a
two-hour distance north from present-day Toronto).

The country of Wendake, which the French visited during
the brief years of existence remaining to it after their arrival
and which they named Huronia,[3] was not a large territory but
possessed unique geopolitical importance since it was situated
at the crossroads of the trade routes going east, west, north,
and south. Upon the arrival of Samuel de Champlain in their
midst in 1610, the Wendat, numbering about 30,000 souls,
had an estimated twenty-five towns, villages, and hamlets (as
reckoned by the French missionaries) spread out over the whole
extent of that small country (roughly 544 square kilometres)
and not alongside the riverways or the shores of lakes, as was
the case for all other Aboriginal nations then living on the
remainder of the now-named Canadian territory. Moreover, the
Wendat had, since at least two centuries prior to the arrival of
Europeans, formed themselves into a powerful Confederacy,
which was itself the commercial and political centre of an
Aboriginal Commonwealth uniting hundreds of nations, large
and small, of the eastern woodlands. We have there, brushed in
large strokes, the portrait of the "Native Commonwealth" that
constituted the strength and power of the overall Native civilization of the Northeast and that became the commercial and
political fundament that France acquired through the alliance
she judiciously made with this very important body of peoples,
at the beginning of the seventeenth century.

That great and ancient Society of Aboriginal Nations,
whose Wendat heart was situated in present-day Canada,
was rapidly and radically destroyed within the thirty or so
brief years following Champlain's first visit. Not so much
by the utterly destructive European diseases or through

wars made intense because of the same European arrival, but as a consequence of France's social backwardness in relation to its Dutch colonial competitor. Indeed, while the French encumbered their Nadowek and Algonquian allies with strict religious conditions when in need of firearms and other metal implements for their defence, the Dutch sold guns liberally to the Hodenosaunee (Iroquois). On the eve of their final dispersal, in 1649, the Wendat still had few arms with which to defend themselves against the Dutch-Hodenosaunee alliance. "The death knell of the great Wendat trading system was sounded on 7 April 1648, when the Governor of New Netherland, Peter Stuyvesant, officially authorized the sale of 400 guns to the Mohawk at an outrageously low price. In 1649, the Hodenosaunee came to disperse the Wendat country, already in ruins."[4]

Before going into the demographic and political situation of the Hodenosaunee at the time of the destruction of the geopolitical order in the Northeast, it is necessary to establish that the Iroquois who lived after this tragic Amerindian collapse of the seventeenth century became, through the power to incorporate by capture and adoption resulting from superior access to European firearms, an amalgam made up of an important number of surviving Aboriginal entities, among which were Wendat, Neutral, Erie, Tionontati, and Susquehanna (Nations and Confederacies now almost all entirely disappeared, with the exception of a few Huron-Wendat and Wyandot communities in Canada and the United States), as well as Algonquians of many different nations.

At the beginning of the seventeenth century, the Hodenosaunee were a relatively new Confederacy. Several versions of the oral tradition of the Hodenosaunee inform us that their Confederacy was the product of the vision of a Huron prophet 'whose message his own people did not want to heed' and who went to the Hodenosaunee country, in present-day New York State, to deliver his message of peace and concord, thereby succeeding in putting an end to a prolonged period of endemic warfare amongst them. Despite this new climate of peace within their Confederacy, the historic Iroquois were made up of only five nations, were not particularly populous, and were deprived of external political or commercial relations, which means they were almost surrounded by enemies, most of whom were numerous and powerful. The Five Nations were confined to themselves and knew little of the art of external trade. One could affirm that had the Europeans not arrived, the logic of the evolution of their society would have been to gradually integrate into the general trading order that had been flourishing in the Northeast for several centuries already. The coming among them of the Wendat Peacemaker, Deganawidah, can be seen as a sign heralding such eventual development.

Our Canadian history books have taught us and, quite regrettably, continue to teach us that the good, docile Hurons were exterminated by the evil, irrational Iroquois. Apparently these two sets of peoples did not have a dream dearer than to destroy each other; consequently, this shared desire would have been realized at any rate so that the Europeans' presence and actions have counted for nothing, or very little, in causing the immense human tragedies that this pretended mutual hate brought about. There is in this hideous historiographical forgery such a charge of anti-Aboriginal sentiment that dealing with its social consequences at multiple levels stands as a task that history will take a long time to carry out. Yet, what is at stake is our dignity, indeed, our respectability as a nation, first in our own eyes and then in those of the world at large. Our country, Canada, does not find its origins in the glorious struggle of European ancestors against brutish, perfidious, savage peoples; quite simply, such peoples do not even exist. Rather, our country takes its origin directly from the rich circular thinking of a marvellous, antique Native civilization, which Canada (and Quebec) have yet to discover.

As late world-renowned ethnohistorian Bruce Graham Trigger argued in the second edition of his landmark book *The Huron: Farmers of the North*, the Huron, even shortly before the events that led to their final dispersal, had no reason at all to fear the Iroquois. At the beginning of the book, Trigger conclusively refutes the analysis followed by numerous specialists on the subject of the demographic arrangement of Wendake, the country of the Wendat. Referring to the plurisecular cultural logic in force among this people, Trigger points out that even in the dark hours of their imminent end, these confederated nations keep on working strenuously to uphold the ancestral order of a vast commercial world of which their Confederacy is the centre. Wendake is the heart of a very vast region; it is densely populated and integrally organized for trade with hundreds of allied peoples making up hundreds of thousands of persons, of whom many learn and speak the Wendat language. Iroquoia is a territory closed in on itself with a sparse population of 20,000–30,000 individuals belonging to five nations situated far from each other on the other side of Lake Ontario. Why would the Iroquois then so much aspire to go and exterminate the Huron? And why would the Wendat abandon their central role in their rich trading world to go assuage their own irrepressible thirst for the blood of their Hodenosaunee relatives?

In very concrete historical terms, France committed the mistake of wasting away the enormous political and demographic advantage that the overwhelming number of her Native allies conferred on her. France neglected to assist these allied nations materially and militarily while, at the same time, the Dutch liberally provided the Five Nations of the Hodenosaunee with the wherewithal that, against all odds, made for the defeat of France's crushing power. For their part, Huron and Iroquois made frequent attempts to unite for the protection of their common interests against their fickle, often disloyal European allies; however, the latter, mostly through an expert spying system operated mainly by religious missionaries, almost always succeeded in frustrating the plans of the First Peoples, whichever side they were on – promoting and advancing their own European cause.

Such is the way in which the French religious historians, to fashion history to suit their convenience, have forged the

myth of the destruction of the Hurons by the Iroquois. But
how does such myth weaken the reasons for our pride as
Canadians, as Québécois? I have created the question and so,
will provide the best answer I can offer. First, it is certain that
any process of colonial appropriation must be accompanied
by an ideological (in most cases, "religious") justification. The
"myth of the victorious Iroquois" is but a historiographical
variant, proper to our Canadian context, of such need for
justification. However, it is also in the order of a society's
evolution that such mythology is one day examined in the
light of reason and of the facts. I believe that the period, in
the evolution of our society, of the negation of the historical
role and contribution of the First Peoples (Amerindian, Métis,
and Inuit) is now behind us. If I judge by the attitude and the
thinking of the youths with whom I have had the chance to
interact, especially in my classes on Aboriginal history and
philosophy, the young and the new Canadians, of all possible
origins, simply do not want to passively feel that their country's history (mostly when it concerns the Aboriginal people
and their country's relations with them) is a "set of lies."

This new generation of Canadians, Aboriginal and
non-Aboriginal, is enlightened to learn that their country
was not built thanks to the glorious and saintly toil of settlers who valiantly risked their lives to come here and shed
the light of reason and of a holy faith on the mores of wild
peoples who, up until the arrival of those worthy carriers
of civilization, had had no other cares but to pursue the
animals in the forests to feed themselves and to hunt each
other down for their ultimate pleasure. The young Canadians
whom I am happy to converse with and, on occasion, to
teach, and from whom I also learn a lot are glad and edified
to find out that their country draws its spiritual and philosophical essence from a beautiful, ancient civilization: that
of its First Peoples. Even though it was soon and radically
smothered, that civilization was the foundation upon which
the colonial elites of European countries, while harshly fighting over ill-acquired goods, established the power and the

grandeur they eventually showed. The Nadowek-Algonquian civilization was, and is, the result of the thinking and of the unending, honest work of a myriad of individuals over multiple generations. France was quick in recognizing the immense, rich material potential possessed by the great society of Native nations heiress to that civilization and grafted itself onto it. It is in this initial colonial movement of France that must be seen the genesis of the existence of colonial Canada as we have known it. It is in the study and understanding of the ancient Aboriginal civilization onto which that graft was made that has to be discovered, at last, the true nature, the real potential, in one word, the soul of our marvellous county, Canada.

The third and last piece is taken from my book *Huron-Wendat: The Heritage of the Circle*. My aim here is to enable my reader to get a feel of the life of the Wendat in their country of Wendake, with some background as to why and how the Wendat came to choose that particular territory. The territory that, for several centuries until the final dispersal of the Wendat Confederacy in 1649–50, constituted the nervous centre of a unique, vast world of trade and alliances. Simultaneously, and even more importantly, I wish to bring you, dear reader, to the realization of what this part of our pre-European Canadian history signifies when we reflect on our deeper Aboriginal social and philosophical legacy, as a country.

The third text:

WENDAKE, LAND OF THE WENDAT

The most likely meanings for the word *Wendake* are "the island apart," "the separate country," "the peninsula country," "the country with a separate language," or, as suggested by renowned geographer Conrad Heidenreich in his landmark book *Huronia*, "the One Village."

Wendake is basically a massive point of land jutting out into Georgian Bay and opening into Lake Huron (where the

largest freshwater island in the world, Manitoulin Island, is
located). This point of land, the Penetanguishene Peninsula,
is shaped like a dog's head with the mouth corresponding to
Penetang Bay.

This country of Wendake was not large. Its twenty to twenty-
five towns, villages, and hamlets were concentrated in a territory measuring about fifty-six kilometres from east to west
and thirty-two kilometres from north to south, bordered by
Matchedash Bay in the north, Nottawasaga Bay in the west,
and Lake Simcoe in the east. On its southern border, the allu-
vial basin of the Nottawasaga River at that time formed a large
swampy zone cutting Wendake off from the territory further
south and reinforcing its island nature. Although this was one
of the most densely populated territories north of Mexico, it
still had enormous potential for demographic expansion.

The five Wendat Nations of the years 1630–40 shared the
territory as follows. The Attignawantan, the principal Nation,
occupied most of the western section; their immediate neighbours were the Ataronchronon to the east with access to
Matchedash Bay, and the Tahontaenrat to the south, mainly in
the interior. The Attigneenongnahac occupied a large territory
with access to Lake Simcoe to the east. The Arendahronon
territory, a rich hunting ground, lay along the northern border.
It ran from Lake Couchiching to Matchedash Bay, benefiting
from the excellent river system draining into the latter, and
continued along the southwest shore of the bay.

The first observers often described Wendake's great beauty.
Nature, they felt, had been exceptionally generous. The
impression given by Champlain's accounts is that of a veritable earthly paradise, particularly in terms of food sources. The
country "abounds" in nature's resources, which are "marvellously good." It is described as "very pleasant in contrast to
such a bad country as that through which we had just come,"
that is, the hunting grounds of the Algoumequins, Nipissings,
and Montagnais. The country is "very fine," Champlain
repeats, "mostly cleared, with many hills and several streams,
which make it an agreeable district." Speaking of the welcome

given him by the Wendat on this first visit, in 1615, he says, "The inhabitants of the villages of Touaguainchain and Tequenonquiaye received us very kindly, giving us the best cheer they could with their Indian corn served in various ways. This country is so very fine and fertile that it is a pleasure to travel about in it."

Champlain was astonished at the luxuriant vegetation. "There is abundance of vines and plums, which are very good, raspberries, strawberries, small wild apples, walnuts, and a kind of fruit of the shape and colour of small lemons ... Oaks, elms, and beeches are numerous there, and in the interior are many plantations of fir-trees, which are the usual retreat of partridges and hares. There are also quantities of small cherries and wild ones, and the same varieties of trees that we have in our forests in France are found in this country."

Eight years later, [Recollet Friar Gabriel] Sagard also commented, "The country is full of fine hills, open fields, and very beautiful broad meadows." He speaks as though personifying the country, which grieves at not being better utilized, then writes: "There is much uncultivated wheat, which has an ear like rye and grains like oats. I was deceived by it, supposing when I first saw it that these were fields that had been sown with good grain. I was also mistaken in the wild peas, which in some places are as thick as if they had been sown and cultivated; and, as a demonstration of the richness of the soil, where a savage of Toënchen had planted a few peas brought from the trading place, they produced peas twice as big as usual, which astonished me, for I had seen none so big either in France or in Canada."

Curiously enough for a cleric, when Sagard speaks of the quality of the Wendat's native soil he is often less fervent and more frankly practical than Champlain. He writes, "There are fine forests, consisting of great oaks, beeches, maples, cedars, spruces, yews, and other kinds of trees, far finer beyond comparison than in the other provinces of Canada that we have seen. Moreover, the country is warmer and more beautiful, and the soil is richer and better the further south one goes.

As Champlain rightly noted, the soil of the ancient Wendat country was mainly sandy, but it was admirably suited to Nadouek corn growing methods. From the standpoint of modern agronomy, Wendake's agricultural and commercial vocations are amply justified in terms of producing surpluses for trade with its Algonquian neighbours, who in turn supplied pelts that the Wendat then traded in the fur market created by the advent of Europeans.

The Wendat trading pattern required large production surpluses, especially of corn, but also of beans and squash. Heidenreich and Fenton have estimated that to feed their 21,000 to 22,500 people (a low estimate), the Wendat had to cultivate between 6,500 and 7,000 acres. Trigger observed that these figures do not take into account the Wendat's trading practices (nor their habit of stockpiling considerable quantities of food underground in their houses, in anticipation of drought years). Trigger also wrote that of all the northern Nadouek, the Wendat, and their Seneca neighbours depended most on agriculture for subsistence.

What makes Wendake so exceptional, compared to any other Amerindian territory, in terms of agricultural production is its close economic ties with its northern neighbours. The *Jesuit Relations* inform us that the Wendat country was "a veritable granary for the Algonquians" (JR 8: 115), as well as a meeting ground. Algonquian groups consisting of hundreds of people would even come south to winter over with the Wendat.[5]

Historian Matthew J. Dennis noted that in Wendake, where corn growing was even more intensive than in Iroquoia, fields became so large that one Jesuit missionary said it was easier to get lost in them than in the neighbouring forests and grasslands. The cornfields seemed like a maze of paths running through an interminable forest of plants easily taller than a man.

The sandy soils of Wendake with their poor moisture retention meant that drought was a continual threat. To forestall shortages, the Wendat kept food reserves to insure against two or more years of poor harvests. The threat was somewhat allayed by the fact that Wendake had five rivers and an infinite number of streams, as Champlain himself noted in 1615.

Climate

Heidenreich estimated that Wendake's climate was the same in the seventeenth century as it is today. With a growing season of 195 days and a frost-free period of 130 to 142 days, the territory was remarkably well suited to growing corn, bean, and squash, the [Nadouek] "three sisters" present in all the horticultural nations of North America.

"Drought was as probable then as now," writes Heidenreich, noting that the five periods of drought recorded by the Jesuits during their nineteen years in the Wendat country conform to present-day observations. For a granular soil, the annual rainfall of seventy-five to ninety centimetres means a slight lack of moisture. Heidenreich feels that severe shortages were a fairly regular feature of life in Wendake, unlike Trigger, who considers that the famine resulting from such droughts was a new phenomenon in the seventeenth century brought on by the combined stress of epidemics that decimated the population, and by the Wendat's new economic obligation to trade almost all their agricultural surpluses. The loss of the 1649 harvest on Gahoendoe Island was thus all the more tragic and fatal for the Wendat because of their complete lack of food reserves.

Accounts of the number of villages in Wendake varied according to the period when European observers were present, or to a given individual's idea of what constituted a village. Champlain counted eighteen villages, Sagard twenty-five, and the Jesuits some twenty. On 17 August 1615, Champlain says he reached Cahiagué, the principal town of the country (probably Arendahronon territory), which he describes as having 200 fairly large houses. It is ... estimated that six Wendat towns had a population of nearly 2,000 or slightly more in the period between 1615 and 1649.

Canada, the Wendat village

Domagaya and Taignoagny, the two Stadaconans captured by
Cartier in the Gaspé harbour in July 1534 and subsequently
taken to France, returned to their own land a year later to
serve as guides for the explorer. They saw their home town,
Stadacona, on 7 September 1535, after spending eight weeks
helping Cartier reconnoiter the countryside from Blanc-
Sablon to Quebec City. Cartier's two guides showed him the
site of their town and spoke of it using the word *Canada*
(spelled variously as Kanatha, Kandatha, and Kanata), which,
in almost all Nadouek languages, simply means Chief-town,
or large village.

Cartier recognized the site's geopolitical importance
to the Amerindians. Coming from monarchic, feudal
Europe, he thought Canada was the centre of a wilderness
empire that he called the *Royaume de Canada*, that is, the
Kingdom of Canada. Donnacona, as Agouhanna or Head
Chief of Stadacona, was branded as being the *Seigneur de
Canada*, at least for the purposes of Cartier's writings. Such,
we may note in passing, was the historic destiny in North
America of the Nadouek word for so simple a concept as
"large village."

Let us see how the Wendat viewed the material aspect of life
in their *canadas*. It is not unrealistic to say that in both their
physical organization and social vision, the Wendat were naturally inclined to take the beaver as their model. This animal
was their political emblem, and as Réal Ouellet points out in
his edition of the works of Baron de Lahontan, they adhered
faithfully to it in constructing the concrete and abstract
aspects of life.

Like all Amerindians familiar with the beaver, the Wendat
viewed it as a sedentary animal that builds and defends
villages, at the same time creating spaces where almost all
other animal species can foregather. Where beaver villages
or colonies exist, waterfowl abound, as well as wetland
animals such as ondathra (muskrats). Deer, elk, and moose

come to drink and feed on plants rarely found elsewhere. Trout swim here, and predators of all kinds come for an easy hunt – above all, human predators, who not only scientifically control the density of the beaver population but also use the environment created by the beaver's labour to cultivate local flora and fauna. "Without the beaver there's nothing: no beaver means poverty for the Indian" is a typical remark made to me by Chief Jean Raphaël, an old late Innu (Montagnais) hunter.

Like the beaver lodge and, symbolically, the beaver village, Wendake itself was an "island" made up of many villages that in turn contained many longhouses or "cabanes," as the Jesuits described them. Wendake was a permanent island-village, a heartland around which revolved a huge world, for the macrocosm of the Amerindian Northeast can be seen as essentially a projection of the Wendat microcosm. This world possessed an ideology that was reflected in Wendat social practice. While the Hodenosaunee advocated the peaceful coming together of all human nations within the Iroquois Longhouse, it was, in fact, Wendake, with its Universal Village, that gave most concrete expression to this philosophical idea.

"BEAVER, EMBLEM OF THE WENDAT"

Like the Beaver, we used to live,
Our houses were of bark and wood;
We built our towns just as they did:
In industry and peace, they stood.
    A special Gift to the Wendat,
    A special Friend to imitate;
    A Provider, but more than that:
    A true Model to cultivate.
  Through Him, we were given the laws
That must govern this Great Island
To make it perfect as It was
When men were One and One, the Land.

O! Dodayeh,[6] to us You were
A living University,
Where each had to become Doctor
In every useful Faculty
Of all the arts, the Ultimate,
You taught us the Art of Living
And the science most Consummate
Of how to live by one's Giving.
        One day, the Sun did not come back;
T' was said He was stricken by shame.
The boats landed, the men wore black.
Many were sick, many were lame.
We gave them a new Breath of Life
And observed them swear to their cross
That they would use poison and knife
To end our World they deemed Chaos.

Like the Beavers, we could not hide;
Trapped were our souls, gotten their furs.
What are now men, without that Guide?
Without use for His protectors?

November 1979

CONCLUSION

In this section, I have wanted to give to my fellow Canadians, to you, my dear reader and relative, a few essential secrets about Canada's history as a way of understanding her deep ideological and spiritual nature and, therefore, what must be its place and its role among the peoples and nations of the world in times to come. I have put forth that Canada, and no other nation created by man on this sacred American soil, our common Mother Earth, our Eatenonha, is heiress to the Native civilization that has given the world the idea of what a global civilization must be, I mean, continentally, the American civilization. I have named that Native civilization the Nadowek-Algonquian civilization

and I have proposed that it was Aboriginally vested in the
Wendat people and Confederacy whose history and political role
I have described in some detail. This implies that the Nadowek-
Algonquian civilization is ancestor to the other Nadowek peoples
and Confederacies, including the Hodenosaunee and, therefore,
that the ultimate true origin of modern American democracy is to
be found in the society of nations that made up this Native civilization to which Canada herself traces its genesis and its existence
as a nation.

Another secret I have been sharing in this present section is that
Canada, and by extension North America as a whole, originates
in a civilization that in remote, pre-European times founded its
ideology and social mores not on aggression and conquest through
violence and conflict but on trade, interculturality, and peace.

As the inheritor of such precious wealth coming from its immemorial past, Canada must be cognizant of, in all intellectual and
practical domains, the Aboriginal ideological and spiritual legacies
which she harbours. Canada has it in her to become a continental
and world model for "americization" that is, for the never-ending
evolution of our human understanding of the idea of "democracy"
and our human obligation to extend this democracy to all the peoples that constitute the universal Circle of Life and are, like us,
children of our sacred Mother the Earth, our Eatenonha.

An even more essential secret to be yet more amply talked
about in this whole essay is how, in concrete political and social
terms, the human peoples we have been speaking about have
gone about creating balance and order in their own world.

Essentially, this ultimate secret is about Earth-centredness and
in practical human terms, mother-centredness.

CHAPTER SIX

EATENONHA:
NATIVE ROOTS OF MODERN DEMOCRACY

The Huron are probably one of the few nations in the world where not a single instance of wife abuse was ever reported. It was simply impossible in this type of society for a man to abuse his spouse.
        Bruce G. Trigger, *Kanata: The Legacy of the Children of Aataentsic*

People in Canada and most certainly students in Indigenous Studies classes are now much more informed about the violence chronically and still customarily endured by Aboriginal women. It is now common knowledge, in our country and beyond, that racial discrimination and its attendant violence principally affect and afflict the Native women (and consequently, their children) caught in those colonial contexts. It is also becoming better known that, sadly, part of that violence is the deed of Native men who are themselves victims of the same colonial social and mental conditioning that engenders the violence against women and, as we shall discuss momentarily, against the Earth, our Eatenonha.

In my lectures, I use this previous quote of Bruce Trigger, taken from the video documentary *Kanata,* and pose the question: How and why have Aboriginal societies, not long ago so exemplarily free of violence against women, now become so markedly gripped by such calamity? Of course, the other question logical in an educational context: Might we very possibly be in the presence of a very rich new field of study? Should we propose to methodically and scientifically find out about how these ancestral societies went about constructing themselves in ways that forestalled the possibilities of social aberrations, such as the gendered violence against women, of ever coming to exist among them?

MATRICENTRISM: WOMEN ARE THE EARTH

The fallout from not living in harmony with our traditions and Mother Earth is borne by the women.
Cree Métis Elder Asisikoowatwaapiskosis (Bernice Hammersmith),
Restoring Women's Value

Matricentric thinking is common to the First Peoples of Canada and, as I and others have proposed, the First Peoples of America. The Wendat, to be sure, share that way of understanding life and the world.

Women are the first environment. We are an embodiment of our Mother Earth. From the bodies of women flows the relationship of the generations both to society and to the natural world. With our bodies we nourish, sustain, and create connected relationships and interdependence. In this way the Earth is our Mother, our ancestors said. In this way we, the women, are Earth.[1]

My aim in proposing the term *matricentrism*[2] is to restore the (antique) notion that, in the natural order, women (and generally, females in the non-human realm) are designed to occupy the central place in their group, or community. This implies that the natural complementarity between the two sexes can only exist when women occupy the centre place in their society. It also implies the idea that in a world vastly become patriarchal the men have invented means, mostly through the use of force – physical, financial, or otherwise – to substitute themselves for the women in the central place of their society. This is, in my view, the seed of the disorder that affects our modern world; we, as a global society, must search in the wisdom of all our respective pasts the ideological and spiritual means for allowing women to regain and occupy the place that belongs to them, that have made possible our existence as humans and that will allow us to keep imagining and constructing our future, as a species.

> [The one-day fast at the age of seven] is a time when the child learns to let go of his/her mother and the mother also learns to let go of her child when the child is put out in the bush to be cradled by Mother Earth. The child is taught that the physical mother is not his/her real mother, but only the mother who cares for, teaches, and guides the child. The child learns who his/her real mother is, and that is Mother Earth. She/he begins the process of learning to respect the Earth for its teachings and spirituality. Mother Earth is the child's first teacher and all things upon Mother Earth are considered sacred. Mother Earth must be treated with respect and kindness, as our Mothers and Grandmothers, for they are life carriers who bring new life into this universe.[3]

The main notion implied in the word matricentrism is that men and women are by nature complementary of each other. While it is a widely acknowledged fact that Aboriginal and Indigenous women on a world scale still hold a place of importance in their own society, people in general and even scholars almost universally use the term *matriarchal* when describing that intriguing trait possessed by these Aboriginal societies. As the Latin and Greek etymology indicates, a *matriarchal* society would be one where the women would be the sex exercising domination over the other. Besides giving an erroneous idea of the traditional functioning of an Aboriginal society, the (generalized) sense given to the idea of matriarchy has the other unfortunate effect of implying that the negative view and the attendant violence done to women under patriarchal rule is quite likely the lesser of two evils since so many societies live and thrive under the patriarchal order. Also, there is the widespread (patriarchal) notion that the age of matricentrism, in spite of some universal qualities it has had in its time including "freedom and equality [for all], kindness to strangers, aversion to restrictions of any kind ... continence and peace,"[4] is but a stage in human evolution and must inexorably and perforce give way to the stage of social maturity in the human order, that is, patriarchy.

MATRILINEAL AND PATRILINEAL SOCIETIES

The term *matrilineal* and its counterpart *patrilineal* often cause confusion. A great many Aboriginal societies the world over have been (and many still are) matrilineal,[5] which the Webster's New World Dictionary defines as "designating of descent, kinship, or derivation through the mother instead of the father." Indeed, the vast majority of the sedentary or semi-sedentary tribes of not only our North American but also our Central and South American continent have existed for millennia according to the matrilineal model. As we have intimated in the preceding lines, this model, where women are at their nature-ordained place at the centre of their society, is the only model whereby a human society can be viably created and prosper. The confusion in the terminology comes when one looks at non-sedentary groups. For such small, nomadic societies who hunt, fish, and collect wild fruits and plants as they travel throughout vast expanses of land, it is plainly observable that the men have the primary role in deciding when and how groups, made up of a few families, will go about securing their subsistence. However, the fact that these patrilineal groupings have been, and continue to be matricentric is recognized not only by the oral tradition of such communities but also by the science of anthropology. Most, if not all nomadic Amerindian societies are, therefore, matricentric even though they are patrilineal and patrilocal (the family lives in the paternal house and community).

THE CIRCLE

There is a common saying among Aboriginal people and scholars of the Aboriginal/Indigenous world: We all come from the Circle, the Circle belongs to no particular people. Typically, one of our highly respected Elders and scholars, Rarihokwats, a Mohawk by adoption, asks students in our Indigenous Studies classes if they are Indigenous. The vast majority truthfully answer: "No, I am a non-Indigenous person, a non-Aboriginal Canadian." The Elder then explains that we are all born Indigenous, that all children are able to "think Indigenous," that is, to see life as a whole, a circle of beings of many sorts and species but all interconnected, all dependent on one another as offspring of their common Mother, the Earth. Then, the Elder asks the class: "If you were born not so long ago, how did you become non-Indigenous?" Of course, Rarihokwats's purpose is to make students reflect on what happens in our modern society to make us lose so early and, generally, so much of the original sensitivity for life that we are all born with. Could it be that in our processes of educating our citizens, we simply have come to leave out how to also educate our hearts and souls?

As we have previously intimated, dear reader, the patriarchal societies we currently live in are, by nature, incapable of imparting in their citizenries the kind of sensitivity for life that we are presently contemplating. The Circle is the woman's domain. Growing up and living within our present social structures, people are systemically made to lose their innate sensitivity for life in its myriad of expressions and forms. The spiritual dimension is abandoned and forgotten. The human community is dissolved. The individual is now the centre; value is placed on the material. The sacredness of each being as part of the universal sacred circle of relations is now irrelevant in the great individualistic free-for-all of transforming everything and anything into money and personal power, which always end up concentrated in the hands of a select few.

GEOGYNOPHOBIA[6]

There is a direct ideological association to be made between the violence done to the Earth and the violence done to women. The word I just wrote, *geogynophobia*, means to convey just that idea. It is composed of three words from the Ancient Greek: *geo*, from *gê*, meaning the earth; *gyno*, from *gynê*, meaning woman, and *phobia*, meaning fear, dread, and/or hatred. The idea behind the word is to help formulate questions about the root causes of the phenomenon of generalized violence against all femininity in the worldwide patriarchal/patricentric culture. When one thinks of patriarchy, one habitually thinks about socio-political systems and about religions. There is now available an increasing quantity of written and audio-visual documents and sources that directly and very often brilliantly expose the ugly reality of the absolutely fright-ful damage being done to the Earth – our Mother, our Eatenonha. This present work, in fact, humbly pretends to be one such attempt to offer our Canadian and global society an "old Huron medicine" to help cure basic woes that we face, all together. As has become evident in this present section and throughout this essay, one of the basic ideas I am wishing to help the community develop further is that one of our strongest hopes lies in our awareness and our ability to restore the place of centrality, dignity, and respect that by nature belongs to women. The corollary that doing this is not a mere matter of social and environmental justice: it is likely that in that idea rests our best chance of finding our survival, our security, and our future prosperity as the human species.

I am proposing a brief digression on the need I perceive for our world to shift away from a blind fixation on religions (all state religions belong to the realm of the patriarchy and have greatly contributed thus far to the breaking up of the great circle of all life). Instead, as is customary in my own Indigenous world, I am proposing some thinking through which religions may find reason to return to their (ab)original purpose, that is, to acknowledge the sacredness of all beings in creation and to practice the ways of love and faith contained in the original teachings of all religions.

Through the years, I have had countless exchanges with people and students of every origin and, to be sure, with the women who have been close to me, such as my maternal grandmother and my mother, and those who are still present in my life, such as my two beloved sisters, Carole and Danyelle, and most especially my so dear life-companion Bárbara. The questions that have most con-stantly recurred during these exchanges and conversations are: Why are men in patriarchal social contexts so prone to exercise violence against women? Is it because men generally hate women, or simply because they want to feel superior? Or, is it because, as some religions predicate, women have caused humanity's fall from grace in the eyes of the Supreme Being and have thus caused man to be forever expelled from the Earthly Paradise? In my manner of thinking, the most likely answer lies in the idea that when humans become estranged from Nature, man begins to look at the Earth and women as things to be owned and exploited for profit and for power. Men, owing their life and their well-being to the Earth and to women, thus begin to feel guilty for their senseless, destructive behaviour in relation to all femininity and the natural consequence is that fear starts dwelling in the hearts of men. In brief, men naturally know that the powers possessed by women are what make their existence and their happiness possible. At the same time, men are assured, through their religions, that they are entitled to own and harness those powers possessed by women. Men, therefore, behave as the proprietors of women (and of the Earth's "natural resources"). The two halves of one same organic unit (man and his complement) have thus become separated and fear and violence have become the fundament of their relationship. Here is my brief digression on matricentrism, patricentrism, religion, and spirituality:

Religions have to go back to their spiritual principles. What the world needs now is spirituality – to arrive at a higher level of consciousness. Religions imply a world where there is a constant state of war against women and against all femininity. Women do not make war against men: it is always the opposite.

Religions enable men to usurp the place of women, which is at the centre, as co-creators and co-originators of societies.

Religions put men at the centre, where they will always attempt to own the power of women. Women, the prime originators of society, are thus forcibly converted into a resource to be harnessed by men.

A permanent state of war against women is thus created where, through violence in many forms and the use of brutal force, women give up their power to men. Patricentrism has thus replaced matricentrism: society, in its natural, mother-centred nature, can no longer be generated. Through their man-made religions, men can convince themselves that the Earth (and all the beings that She creates and nurtures) must be harnessed as a source of resources and converted into power to be used for themselves. Violence and brutality, sanctioned by religions, become the prescribed way of creating and ordering societies.

Principles of education and civility are defined and ingrained at a young age in citizens to desensitize humans and society about the life-destructive manners in which men create, obtain, and exercise their power. Religions must go back to their spiritual, matricentrist, and life-enhancing principles so that we can find again the great, sacred Circle of Life and heal ourselves, as humans.

LEADING IN A CIRCULAR-THINKING SOCIETY

In approaching this topic, I must emphasize that our goal in this essay is not to suggest that the ideas expounded here have applicability in our present-day social context: they have limited practical value in our current reality and will need long and very serious attention and examination at all levels in our educational system and in our social institutions. Rather, our purpose is to bring out those ideas – political, social, and otherwise – developed by our Aboriginal Peoples long before Canada came to exist and to offer those deeply Canadian ideas as food for reflection for the public at large, as well as a pertinent subject of study for the scholarly and artistic worlds. Our purpose, indeed, is none less than to affirm and explain why and how *the true roots of democracy itself are deeply, authentically, and Aboriginally Canadian.* One of the most profound and most meaningful differences between the two civilizations we are contemplating is to be found in the way each of them chooses its leaders and governs itself.

Rarihokwats, echoing so many sages, shares some of his Mohawk wisdom: Any society where men are free to choose leaders among themselves is bound to produce disunity, systemic injustice, abuse of women and children and of the environment, poverty, uncontrollable levels of criminality, and generalized disorder.

Rarihokwats also reminds us that traditional Native wisdom dictates that a man perceived by the community as "wanting to be a leader" will be seen as a risk to the community and thus, will never be chosen to occupy such a position. It is well known that in traditional Aboriginal (matricentric) societies, leaders were selected and appointed by the mothers and the councils of the Clan Mothers. First, it must be stated that circular (Aboriginal/ Indigenous) thinkers the world over believe that women are not designed by nature to occupy the positions of leaders in the realm of political and civic affairs; in those societies, women themselves feel and will state clearly and eloquently that they have their own realm of duties and occupations that they feel are as important as those of their men counterparts and have neither the desire nor inclination to go and sit for hours or days in the men's Council Houses.

Generally, the women exercise their authority in the home and in the village (or town segment) and the men's world is everything that is external to the women's domain.[7] There is a simple, obvious explanation of why leaders are chosen (and, always possibly, destituted) by the women in circular-thinking societies. Those boys who will one day become the leaders come to the world born by women and it is those mothers who will principally observe those children and determine which ones possess the special soul and heart qualities that leaders need to have. Those qualities are generosity, humbleness, a marked inclination to renounce self-interest and to serve others, empathy, compassion, and a very high awareness of the spiritual dimension of life. A leader must always be guided by his very nature, by his impeccable sense of respect for all forms and expressions of life, and by his love of others and of his community. As we have said before, dear reader, a patricentric society is neither prone nor able to cultivate and impart this kind of sensitivity to its members. Rather, such a society encourages and rewards competitiveness and individualism. As we have also said, in reason of different evolutionary paths and of constraints thus created in different social contexts and physical environments (and not because of any ill-disposition present in their social makeup as it has evolved), the Circle for such societies has vanished as a spiritual and ideological reality and has been replaced by the Line.

CANADA'S FIRST CIVILIZATION AS INSPIRATION
FOR A FUTURE WORLD ORDER

We have described in some detail how a pre-European Indigenous Commonwealth, of which the Wendat Confederacy was the geopolitical centre, was the foundation upon which our country and, through the vicissitudes of history as it unfolded, our neighbour to the south, the United States of America, came to exist. It is my proposition that the sum of the political and cultural ideas elaborated over time by that extended multi-cultural, multi-lingual society can offer thought models of high relevancy for the world that we, modern humans, ambition to create for our future.

George and Louise Spindler, anthropologists from Stanford University wrote in their preface to Bruce Trigger's second edition of his landmark book *The Huron: Farmers of the North* that

> particularly notable in the author's reconstruction of the Huron way of life is their preoccupation with personal independence and economic equality. Huron culture contained an "elaborate set of positive and negative social sanctions which served to inhibit the development of economic and political inequality." This characterization raises serious questions about some of the assumptions of an evolutionary model that transforms small interpersonal and group differences into classes and ranks with power wielded by a few individuals.
>
> There are many aspects of Huron culture and society that impress us as anthropologists. Particularly impressive to us as psychological anthropologists are the culturally patterned techniques in Huron culture for maintaining individual balance. The culture provided channels through which idiosyncratic needs of individuals could be met, sometimes in a spectacular manner and often in ways that transgressed normal sanctions or behaviour. As students of Native American culture, we view the *inventions* [my italics] by others for the maintenance of psychic security and personal satisfaction with special interest.
>
> In this and other ways we may see in Huron culture, as remote in time and origin from our own as it is, a reflection of

our common human and contemporary problems. The Huron
solved these problems in their own unique manner but is ways
recognizable to us.[8]

Again, central to our present discussion on how and why certain
Wendat sociological "inventions" have potential relevance for our
modern world contexts is the subject of who the Wendat chose to
be their leaders. As we already know, it was the women (mothers
and Clan Mothers) who chose, appointed, and (possibly) destituted the leaders. This brings us back to our central topic for this
section: matricentrism and circular thinking and the way society
was organized and functioned under this kind of social system.
First, I will bring out from a few sources on the Huron the fact
that the Huron example stands in contradiction to the patriarchal
notion that woman is naturally subservient to man.

Sociologist Maurice Godelier has suggested that the subor-
dination of woman to man has always existed and continues
to exist in all present-day societies. Karen Lee Anderson,
also a sociologist (University of Toronto), offers a contrary
view, based on ethnohistorical and archaeological evidence
of Wendat society. As members of a matrilineal, matrilocal
society whose subsistence economy was based on horticul-
ture, fishing, hunting, and trade, Wendat women appear,
from all historical accounts, to have been extraordinarily
free of male domination.

The Jesuit Joseph-François Lafitau, who worked as a missionary among the Iroquois in the early eighteenth century,
also knew the Wendat intimately. His *Moeurs des Sauvages
Américains* gives the impression that, for all practical purposes,
men did not exercise definitive power in these Aboriginal
societies. He pointed out that women were the real backbone
of the nation. Family lines and genealogy were traced through
women, as was "noblesse" (nobility). They wielded effective
authority, being in charge of the earth, the fields, and the crops.
Women were "the soul of the councils and the arbiters of peace
and war," and it was to them that captives were awarded. They

controlled the wealth of the community; they arranged marriages and were the custodians of children (and through them
controlled inheritances).[9]

GOVERNMENT, LAW, AND POWER

In closing this section, I will use segments of a discussion to be
found in its entirety in my book *Huron-Wendat. The Heritage
of the Circle*. In it, I have relied substantially on the art and the
knowledge of Bruce Graham Trigger, the foremost, irreplaceable
authority on the Wendat. First, we see how a Circle society has a
natural propensity to avoid centralization of power. As well, we are
given by a Jesuit missionary an illustration of how a (matricentric)
society factually instills in its members a high degree of empathy
and sensitivity for others.

In Circle societies mutual respect and recognition must always
exist among members. This makes it possible to apply the law
of consensus, as opposed to the coercive authority invested by
linear societies in, for example, a police force. However, a society in which the law of consensus applies cannot become too
large. Once it reaches a certain size, it breaks up into subgroups
in order to preserve a high degree of social cohesion within each
community. Speaking of this latent tendency for Wendat communities to subdivide, geographer Conrad Heidenreich explains that
"village co-operation increases as population numbers decrease,
and lack of co-operation increases when more and more people
are involved." He feels that the Wendat (as well as their neighbours) did not have the social mechanisms (such as coercion by
police) to cope with large numbers of people if these did not wish
to co-operate. However, if we look at the question from the circular perspective, we see a society of people unaccustomed to
compromising their individual or group independence – a society that must have developed an instinct to subdivide when the
need became apparent. There was, as a rule, no intention of making a definitive break; on the contrary, the aim of regrouping
in a smaller unit was to prevent relationships from deteriorat-
ing, thereby preserving the basic unity that all Wendat took for

granted. The virtues of this social art did not escape the Jesuits, who in 1636 remarked on Wendat government as follows:

> They have a gentleness almost incredible for savages. They are not easily annoyed, and moreover, if they have received wrong from anyone they often conceal the resentment they feel — at least, one finds here very few who make a public display of anger and vengeance. They maintain themselves in this perfect harmony by frequent visits; by help they give one another in times of sickness, by feasts and by alliances. When they are not busy with their fields, hunting, fishing, or trading, they are less in their own houses than in those of their friends; if they fall sick, or desire anything for their health, there is a rivalry as to who will show himself most obliging. If they have something better than usual ... they make a feast for their friends, and hardly ever eat it alone.[10]

Next, here are two observations of Trigger on chiefship, on the personal qualities needed to be a Chief, and on some of the social commitments and obligations implicated by such role.

> [Wendat] Chiefs had no constitutional authority to coerce their followers or to force their will on anyone. Moreover, individual Wendats were sensitive about their honour and intolerant of external constraints, and friends and relatives would rally to the support of someone who believed himself insulted by a Chief. Overbearing behaviour by a Chief might, therefore, encourage violent reaction and lead to conflicts within or between lineages. In the long run, Chiefs who behaved arrogantly or foolishly tended to alienate support and would be deposed by their own lineages.[11] The ideal [Wendat] Chief was a wise and brave man who understood his followers and won their support by means of his generosity, persuasiveness, and balanced judgment.[12]

Again, Bruce Trigger on leadership:

Being a Chief, especially a civil Chief (as opposed to Chief of defence, or "war" Chief), required the expenditure of considerable time and wealth. They were expected to entertain their supporters as well as to provide hospitality for visitors. They also had to travel considerable distances to attend meetings, sometimes in very bad weather. The Chief at whose house a meeting was held was obliged to provide food and entertainment for his visitors. This required him and his family to work harder than anyone else to produce the food that had to be given away to validate his public office. Likewise, most of the goods that Chiefs received as presents or from their control of trade routes had to be given away to maintain the reputation for generosity without which a Chief would have no support. The more influential a Chief, which meant the larger were the number of people in whose name he spoke, the greater was the scale on which he had to provide feasts and give away exotic goods.[13]

Finally, and coming right back to where and when our country, Canada, had its beginning (Quebec City, 1535), I am giving an illustration, here reported by a Recollet missionary, of how these quintessential qualities that constitute a leader found expression in a circular-thinking (matricentric) society, be it sedentary, such as the Stadacona (Nadowek) or nomadic, such as the Mi'kmaq (Algonquian).

Jacques Cartier noted in 1535 that the Stadacona Chief Donnacona, who he styled in his writings "the Lord" or "King of Canada," was no better off than his people, who "live with almost everything in common." In this, he was no different from all other Amerindian Chiefs in the Northeast and in the Americas generally, who only held office by virtue of their capacity and readiness for giving. The Recollet Chrestien Le Clercq detected this spiritual quality in a Micmac (now more accurately named Mi'kmaq) Chief during the 1680s.

He made it a point of honor to be always the worst dressed and to see to it that all his people were better clothed than he,

having as a maxim, so he told me one day, that a Sovereign
and great heart like his should rather care for others than for
himself; because being the good hunter that he was, he would
never have trouble getting everything he needed; that in any
case, if he didn't eat well, he would find what he wished in the
affections and in the hearts of his subjects; as if he wanted to
say that his treasures and wealth were in the hearts and good-
will of his people.[14]

EPILOGUE

In this essay, I have posited that the origins of modern democracy are to be traced back to the "Aboriginal Commonwealth" that began to exist in what are now the eastern woodlands of Canada several centuries before the arrival of Europeans and that we have termed "Canada's first civilization."

This affirmation, as we have also previously seen, stands in contrast to the popular idea that modern liberal democracy originated in the replication by the original Thirteen Colonies that became the United States of America, of the Five Nations (Iroquois) model of confederating various smaller political entities into a larger one that would produce an optimal amount of power for this new, thus constituted state. We have, in this essay, taken the view that *true democracy*, in the sense of recognizing and responding to our global human responsibility of organizing our continued existence and prosperity in this material world of ours, *must be inclusive of all realms of life, human and other-than-human.*

We are now in touch with the heart and soul of our true spiritual legacy, as Canadians. Looking to our future as a country, we Canadians must (and many already do) create around ourselves an educational and a social environment where we are able to love and cherish our land, our living spaces, as our Mother, our Eatenonha. To attain that level of consciousness, which will be the guarantee of our viability and true prosperity for all times to come, we need to reflect and understand how and why our Aboriginal forebears had built their civilizations on the foundations of love, respect, trust, and faith in the spirit of their land. Like them, though in our own time and with our own evolving circumstances, we need to recognize that life, while it needs to be fecundated by male beings, is born in female wombs and that only when women do not get displaced from their own place in the centre of the community but are left free to occupy that natural place of theirs can a human society generate and impart in its members the kind of human sensitivity that makes for the orderly, normal continuation of life itself.

In short, Canada, in order to continue to be the strong, successful, world-inspiring nation that it is, will be well advised to discover and to prize its true Aboriginal spirituality and intellectual heritage. It has become impossible not to see that the time for the linear in our collective evolution is passed. It is exciting to live in a time when we have no choice but to recognize our mutual closeness and our interdependence as a species and as a global family of beings sharing the Great Sacred Circle of Life all together. In the not so distant future, we will come to see and treat our land, our country, *as our Eatenonha, our first and ultimate Mother*. Then will we be able to make our most important contribution to the world as the first and original inheritors of the most authentic tradition of democracy. We will help the world (and also ourselves) understand that there is no democracy outside the Circle and the true democracy is a matricentric miracle born in the bodies and in the spirits of our mothers, of our women. That is the great, ineffable gift contained in the legacy of Canada's first civilization.

Thank you, my dear friends and relatives. Following the way I have learned from my Elders, from my people, I say to you, to all people, from the bottom of my heart: "*I love you. You are my people.*" Etsagon! (Let us take heart and be happy!)

Your brother,
Georges Sioui

PRESENTATION TO THE CALACS (CANADIAN ASSOCIATION FOR LATIN AMERICAN AND CARIBBEAN STUDIES)

Americity: The Integration of the Americas through Their Indigenous Cosmologies

University of Costa Rica, 10 July 2015

Dear friends and relatives, it is most certainly a distinct pleasure and an honour to be back after twenty-one years in this beautiful, enchanting country of Costa Rica, in this dear city of kind, warm-hearted people, which is San José and in this truly great, progressive and welcoming University of Costa Rica. I had then, in October 1994, attended and given a paper at the First Central American Congress of Anthropology. Many things have occurred in my life during those twenty-one years, mostly very positive and beautiful, but one which mostly stands out and which I think worth mentioning is that this time around, I am accompanied by a young scholar and presenter, a human geographer, also my best friend, my son, Miguel Paul Sioui.

AMERICITY, AMÉRICITÉ, AMERICIDADE, AMERICIDAD

There is a new planetary consciousness
Coming from the unification of the four Aboriginal Americas

Há uma nova consciência planetária
Vindo da unificação das quatro Americas autóctoneas

Il y a une nouvelle conscience planétaire
Qui vient de l'unification des quatre Amériques autochtones.

Hay una nueva conciencia planetaria
Viniendo de la unificación de las cuatro Américas autóctonas.

Humanamity!
Humanizade!
Humanamitié!
¡Humanamistad¡

Mother Earth!
Mãe Terra!
Mère Terre!
¡Madre Tierra¡

In my presentation, I would like to offer two concepts which I have created and used for more than three decades in my field of Indigenous history: the concept of "Americity" and the other concept of "the four Americas."

The first, "Americity," implies fostering in our students and in the academe, as well as in our globalized society, an ability to see the American continent through the Indigenous American cosmologies. Like the other continents, America has ways of being and seeing that make it ideologically unique. Daniel Garrison Brinton, the famous US anthropologist, who specialized in the study of the Central American Indigenous cultures and languages, wrote in 1868:

"Cut off time out of mind from the rest of the world, he [the Indigenous American] never underwent those crossings of blood and culture which so modified and on the whole promoted the growth of the old world nationalities. In his own way he worked out his own destiny and what he won was his with a more than ordinary right of ownership."

I and many others also believe and have said and written that because of its isolated geographical situation until relatively very recently, it can be affirmed that the American continent, with the possible addition of Australia, possesses a worldview surpassing in originality that of all other continents. As to the practical and ideological value represented by this properly American philosophical system for the rest of the human community, I am suggesting that ample proof of such value is found in the fact of the irresistible appeal, indeed, the fascination that the American continent has had for countless individuals of all regions of the world, since 1492. The idea of the Noble Redman ("le Bon Sauvage") has existed almost from the very moment Europeans set eyes on the (so-called) New World and began to observe its original inhabitants. For all of mankind, America has always evoked beauty, abundance, freedom, hope, happiness and peace.

Now, what social ethics underlie the unique character of America? An essential trait of that ethics was (and continues to be) that the notion of man's entitlement to divide and possess the Earth was absent in Aboriginal America. Another essential cosmological characteristic was that state (read: patriarchal) religions were not present either (though forms of theocratic systems existed in certain very populated parts). In general terms, through a shared vision of Creation as a universal Circle of relations, peoples and communities acknowledged the physical reality of the Earth, Mother of all and therefore indivisible and property of no one. To be sure, such "circular-thinking," as opposed to "linear-thinking" societies have existed and still exist in every continent; however, I suggest that America, because of its vastness and its geographic isolation, was and still is, "par excellence," the continent where that original form of human thinking and behaving still thrives. Indigenous Americans (Amerindians) felt and lived an integral democracy, inclusive not just of humans, but of all beings of all orders.

Drawing with unrestrained freedom from the apparently limitless material wealth of this vast, new continent, the countries that have formed in it, especially in the northern part, very rapidly came to symbolize for the rest of the world the ultimate model of a successful social and political ideology. Standing on their belief in the inexhaustibility of Nature's wealth and thus in their own greatness, these so-named developed states have had little difficulty in imposing, on a world scale, the political and social way of Americanism. This ideology offers an illusion of material progress, benefitting certain groups in their society while at the same time concealing the destitution of the majorities. This same way of Americanism cannot be dissociated from the attendant misery of the other orders of life comprised under the common appellation of "the environment."

"Americity" finds its opposite in the word "Americanism." Going deeper into the meaning and nature of this linear way of thinking, Americanism is the materialistic, shallow philosophy that the Euroamerican, much more so in the northern part of the continent, historically deprived of access to an intimate, spiritual comprehension of his continent of adoption, has invented and with which he has upheld in the eyes of the world an image of prestige, protective power, indeed, magnanimous generosity. From this viewpoint, Americanism appears as the ideology that has, until now, usurped the true spiritual visage of America, which I am suggesting we name "Americity."

Americity, then, implies the character of a spirituality and thus, of a social ethics that are America's own. It is the consciousness of a power, as well as of a duty belonging to this continent, to define and to offer to the rest of the human and cosmic family a vision of life and of the universe that can help transform our human world into a truly unified, universalized society. Essentially, Americity signifies the formulation, for the benefit of all beings of all orders, of the reasons why and especially, of the the ways how to adopt the circular and matricentric worldview so markedly characteristic of America: we shall see momentarily how these two notions are intimately linked. This worldview has enabled America to be a haven of tolerance and hope for very many human beings.

MATRICENTRISM

As just mentioned, I would now like to speak, briefly, about how the two notions of *circular thinking* and *matricentrism* are closely related, in fact, so much so that they are in many ways synonymous. Taking support in the teachings of many Elders of our Indigenous nations, and other wise people, I have put forth in several of my writings that certain peoples, because of constraints particular to their proper historical trajectory, have come to forget that life is a sacred Circle of relations and to believe that it is instead an evolutionary process which progresses in linear fashion towards an unknown future. I have described this abandonment of the circular thinking as an ideological accident, a sort of derailment from Nature's laws. I have also written that this original thinking way of the human is "matricentrist," which signifies that it is based on the recognition that our happiness, as well as our security as humans depend on our recognizing the filial link which unites us to the Earth, nurturer of our bodies, minds, hearts and spirits.

As we depend on the Earth our Mother for our life and our equilibrium in every way, so do we recognize in our mothers, our wives, our grand-mothers, our aunts, our daughters, our women-companions, this same gift, which women possess, of a special consciousness of the more vital, higher needs of societies and of the ways of meeting those needs. Thus, these original circular-thinking societies have had the ability to create their social and political institutions from a sovereign faith in the sacred gifts of woman, carrier and giver of life. Those societies, globally referred to as Indigenous, that is, non-state societies, are matricentric (even when they are patrilocal and patrilineal), which is to say that they place woman in the center of their thinking and of their sociopolitical organization, contrary to what happens in the linear-thinking societies, which are patricentric and colonial and relegate women to the status of property/producer/reproducer. Men, in linear-thinking societies can thus, with the blessing of patriarcal religions, impunely dominate and exploit women.

THE FOUR AMERICAS

I will now speak a little more of the second concept, "the four Americas." The idea which underlies this concept comes from the observation of the fact that the Indigenous presence, throughout the whole continent of America, is gaining strength. After more than five centuries of being crushed, silenced and thought extinguished forever, the voices of the Indigenous American peoples and nations are making themselves heard, ever louder and clearer. And they are now finding open ears and hearts everywhere, amongst all peoples, here and abroad.

A corollary to the observation just made is that since there is strength in numbers, the Indigenous peoples of the Americas are finding ways to communicate amongst themselves, as well as to converse with the outside world in a unified, universalized manner. Put simply, the idea of the "the four Americas" is to recognize, besides the myriad languages indigenous to America, the four European languages that have taken hold in the American continent, that is, English, French, Portuguese and Spanish, with a view of utilizing them to enable all of America's Indigenous peoples and nations (with the contribution of every other person or group interested) to study, define and share their social, philosophical and spiritual unity (and also, of course, their own respective idiosyncrasies). The end goal is that of helping fulfill the historical role which Indigenous Americans have always seen as their own, that of "Americizing" America and also, making their own unique contribution to the world. "The four Americas" is a discursive tool for effecting the spiritual and intellectual repossession of their continent by the Indigenous Peoples of America. It conveys to these four European Americas that they each are *only one* of four Americas in the eyes of the Indigenous peoples, and it enables all Americans to see and assume the oneness of their continent at the spiritual level.

The idea of "the four Americas" also implies that my Innu and Abnaki brothers and I live in the francophone America; that my Dakota, Dènè and Chippewa relatives inhabit the anglophone America; that our Kogi, Maya, Quechua and Bribri sisters are inheritors of the hispanic America, and our Kayapó, Yanomami and Xavante relatives' second language is Portuguese in their America lusóphona. For us Indigenous Americans, those differences are only accidental and rather than dividing us, help us reach out to one another in our Amerindianness. For Euroamericans generally, these same differences belong to a very serious social mythology. Oppositions have existed, wars have even been waged and dissensions keep being fomented every day in the name of cultural or religious differences, in reality superficial; oppositions, dissensions and wars whose rhetoric never succeeds in hiding the real motive which is the material possession of the territory and of the goods it will produce for the patriarchal elites.

CONCLUSION

To utilize and adopt the Indigenous American self-perception and to see four Americas instead of one (dominated by the United Sates), two (North and South America) or three (North, Central and South) would be for all Americans a way to begin to understand their history and therefore to define the social, economic and political parameters which will enable America to recognize itself collectively and to better preserve and cultivate its own proper role on a world scale in times to come. To adopt a properly American self-perception is, I propose, to begin to discover and to recognize, with affection and empathy, our American family. To see America from an Indigenous vantage point means to enrich and strengthen ourselves with an alternative vision to more efficiently tackle our own American political, social, ecological and other challenges. To give ourselves a properly American social ethics signifies, in the end, disembarking spiritually in the New World and responding to the offer of inclusion and to the smiles of the peoples who had first come down to the shores, ready to welcome and exchange in order to live even better, all together.

I have proposed the term "americity" because of the domineering connotation of the term «americanity," as well as of the verb "americanize" and of the substantive "americanization." "Americity," "americize" and "americization" are the American Indigenous counterparts to those three terms. They imply that the "americanizing" power of the US (and of the North generally) must also be looked at from the American Indigenous peoples' viewpoint. After more than five centuries of americanization of America and the world, there is a powerful world-wide current of thought that indicates it is now time to collectively reflect on the sources and the roots of life itself, which are in the Earth, which is one. We must find the ways to all join together to mend and heal the whole world!

Dear friends and relatives, I thank you wholeheartedly for having listened to me.

Georges Sioui

NOTES

INTRODUCTION

1 For more on this concept, please see Georges Sioui, "The Fourth Family of Nations," in *Histories of Kanatha*, 67–70.

CHAPTER ONE

1 I will give some more details further on.
2 There are other Huron-Wyandot communities in Ontario and in the United States, notably in Kansas and Oklahoma.

CHAPTER TWO

1 The family name *Sioui* comes from the name *Seawi*, or *Tseawi*, and was originally the name of a people belonging to one of the five Nations of the Wendat Confederacy. It refers to the East and means "the people of the rising sun" or, metaphorically, "the ones who hold the light." Kondiaronk, Chief of the Hurons of Detroit, the principal leader in the historic Peace Treaty known as The Great Peace of Montreal that was ratified in 1701 by thirty-nine Aboriginal nations and the French, was a Seawi:aga, that is, a descendant and a member of the Seawi.
2 This story (pages 27–9) is the translation from the French original, taken from my book *Huron-Wendat: The Heritage of the Circle*. (Translator for UBC Press: Jane Brierly.)

3 "Canadiens": we then thus designated the non-Indians. Many of our more northerly friends, mostly the Montagnais (nowadays properly referred to as Innu), used to pronounce, in their own manner of speaking French, "Caniyens." Since then, the "Canadiens" have changed their name to "Québécois." As to the names of the Amerindian nations mentioned here, the trend, after over three decades have passed since the writing of this text, has been to return to the ancestral autonyms of these nations; for example, Wabanaki, Innu, Anishinabe, Atikame'kw, Mi'kmaq, Wuastukwiuk (Maliseet), Eenou/Eeyou (Cree).

4 In French Canadian country language, *campe*, borrowed from the English "camp," designates a log house, usually not of large dimensions.

5 We are in April 1980, four and a half years before my father's passing. I refer my readers to chapter 4 of the present essay where I explain how the Sioui Decision, in 1990, re-established my Huron-Wendat people in the free exercise of certain territorial rights.

Regrettably, my father was no longer there to see his prediction come true (that is, that one day, we would be able to "return home, in the woods"). Since the Sioui Decision, we are no longer seen or treated as outlaws in our own territories. My father lived long enough to witness the beginnings of that legal battle and to inspire us with his rock-solid certainty that "Truth, the daughter of Time, always triumphs in the end." "We will win," he had foretold.

6 We would, in time, also have Hugues and Danielle, born in 1955 and 1957 respectively.

7 As he grew up, Konrad became an athlete and excelled at many sports, notably canoe-racing and ice hockey. He has also left his mark locally, provincially, nationally, and internationally as an Aboriginal political leader. Konrad has now held the position of Grand Chief of our Huron-Wendat Nation for ten years.

8 That visit of our father to our school did much to relieve both of us (as well as other children from traditionalist families) of a burden we had to carry because both of our parents were Indian – a social sin that must be paid dearly in those times

– and because there was talk on the Reserve about my father's drinking, which was one more excuse to reinforce the negative stereotypes we suffered from.

9 Established in 1697, our Reserve has changed names many times. It was first, Attignawantan, or Nation of the Bear; then, Jeune Lorette, or Roreke (Lorette); then, Village-des-Hurons; and finally, in the 1990s, Wendake (roughly pronounced Wondakeh).

10 Today, in our lives as adults and professionals, many of us stand, out of respect, but do not sing. We are waiting for the day when this country, which pretends to include us, will recognize not only with words but with actions our equality, indeed, our right to be, our unique place and role in its midst, as first heirs of the thought-world of its First Peoples.

CHAPTER THREE

1 At this point, I must make clear that the vicissitudes endured historically by the people of the Forty Arpents can now be looked at as "old history"; my purpose in writing this book is not to give those past hardships importance they no longer have. Rather, my primary objective is to enrich my reader with a sense of our country's history that I believe will otherwise remain unknown. I must also express here the pride that I feel to belong to my Huron-Wendat Nation, a modern Canadian Aboriginal community praised and admired by very many people, of all origins, as a worthy, hope-giving example of prosperity, ingenuity, and order, as well as pride in our origins, history, and numerous on-going achievements. My whole-hearted feelings of solidarity and love go out to every member of my Huron-Wendat Nation.

2 Taken from my book *Seawi*.

3 Notably in Fenton, *The Roll Call of the Iroquois Chiefs*.

4 The term *gynocentric* is also employable in this context.

5 The term in Wendat is *Garihoua doutagueta*.

6 The Condolence Ritual is still used to install a Civil Chief in the Hodenosaunee. It is a very solemn ritual that lasts several days.

The *Royaner* thus named becomes one of the (now) forty-nine "Condoled" Chiefs of the League.

7 My reader may wish to read the brief article in Sioui, *Histories of Kanatha*, 223–27.

8 Her words, in French: "Retournons-nous en donc chez-nous."

9 Please see Sioui, "Canada: Its Cradle, Its Name, Its Spirit," in *Histories of Kanatha*, 289–302.

10 A comprehensive study of the history and life of that community is yet to be made. It is my hope that the information given in the present essay will trigger the interest of scholars for this topic.

11 Originally, the Wendat had been a matrilineal society. This term refers to the social organization, common to a great number of Aboriginal peoples, whereby descent is traced through the female line and the leaders are appointed by the Clan Mothers. The term *matricentric* refers to a social philosophy whereby mothers, and women in general, are politically and ideologically positioned in the centre of families, Clans, societies, Nations, and Confederacies.

12 The Forty Arpents community was only one among many traditional Native communities across Canada that governments and churches were intent on legally eliminating during that era.

13 We have briefly touched on this event in a previous chapter: "Hurons of the Rising Sun".

14 Readers wishing to hear Dr Trigger express this assertion can view on YouTube the documentary *Kanata: The legacy of the Children of Aataentsic* (19:00–19:40).

15 My mother received that distinction from the hands of a very great Canadian, former governor general, the Right Honorable Adrienne Clarkson, to whom Éléonore related to as a sister and a friend. To receive her medal, Éléonore was very proud to be accompanied by a son she adopted in her Clan, the great ethnohistorian of the Wendat, Bruce Graham Trigger.

16 A reference to my father's long struggle with alcoholism.

17 To many Aboriginal peoples, including us Wendat, the Creator is a total, perfect entity and is, therefore, both feminine and masculine – both our Father and our Mother.

18 Georges-Albert Sioui was also an excellent hockey and baseball player. He stood out in almost every sport and was especially proud of his local fame as a wrestler.

19 This text can be found online on the site of the University of Innsbruck's Center for Inter-American Studies.

20 That collection was published in 2013 by Dialogos Books, in New Orleans, under the title *Seawi*.

21 My readers may wish to read a brief article in Sioui, "The Fourth Family of Nations," in *Histories of Kanatha*, 67–70.

22 I am now retired, as of December 2016; I, of course, sporadically lecture by invitation.

CHAPTER FOUR

1 Aronia means "the Sky" in Wendat. We are informed by the Jesuits that it was used as a concept to refer to the Creator of all things, the Great Spirit, the Great Mystery.

2 To be sure, we have sister-nations in America who speak Creole languages derived from one, or several, of the four languages that have taken root in this continent (English, French, Portuguese, and Spanish), apart from some ancestral African and Amerindian languages. These nations and peoples are nearly all Métis (*Mestizos* in Spanish; *Mestiços* in Portuguese), that is Aboriginal. For more on "the Four Americas," please refer to the Appendix.

3 The Province of Quebec developed nine arguments in hopes of winning this case. The Province of Quebec was defeated on all counts. The Supreme Court episode lasted three years and research, on our side, took our legal advisors across the Atlantic in order to study British records, especially regarding the strategic intentions of the English in making this Treaty. The Supreme Court's decision was unanimous: nine judges against none (full details on the proceedings are available on the Internet).

Three questions about the Huron-British document formed the basis of the *Sioui* Case:

1 Does the document, signed by General James Murray on 5 September 1760 constitute a Treaty within the meaning of Canada's Indian Act?

2 If the answer to question 1 is in the affirmative, was the Treaty still operative on 29 May 1982, at the time when the alleged offenses were committed?

3 If the answers to questions 1 and 2 are in the affirmative, are the terms of the document of such a nature as to make current, generally applicable laws unenforceable in respect of the respondents?

4 Roy Thomas is the artist who created the painting on the cover of this book.

5 This was turned into a humorous anecdote in the foreword I wrote for Herb's celebrated book *The Hollow Tree*.

6 I must here briefly describe the part played by each one my four brothers in the defence of the case.

Régent was, at the onset and for most of the whole duration of the legal process, the Councillor (our Nation's Council was then made up of eight Councillors, also called Sub-Chiefs) who was instrumental in reversing a decision by our National Council to not support our case; therefore, not allowing money to be disbursed for a legal defence. Régent was able to convince a majority of his fellow-Councillors to appropriate national funds to create from our case a test case for determining the substance and extent of our Nation's rights on the territory in question. The case was thus launched on its legal course.

Konrad was, during the years of our legal battle, Grand Chief for all First Nations in the Province of Quebec and Labrador and second-in-command (after National Chief Georges Erasmus) at the Assembly of First Nations for all of Canada. Konrad fought successfully to gain the support of all of Canada's First Nations, as well as a very large part of the Canadian public. Through his widely acknowledged political skills, he also helped ensure that the country's best lawyers were appointed to the case. Konrad has been the Grand Chief of our Huron-Wendat Nation since 2008.

Hugues was our "Territorial Chief," a great hunter and woodsman who organized the Nation's forces in all matters pertaining to the traditional use of the territory. We lost Hugues, our youngest brother, to cancer four years ago. He shall always be remembered and missed for his wisdom, his courage, and his dedication to his people, as well as for his wits and his keen sense of humour.

Vincent, though not implicated in the case and not formally trained in the legal professions, has been and will continue to be a legal genius of sorts. In the Wendat tradition of old, he is a true strategist and he played a critical role at all stages in our common struggle.

7 I would be remiss if I did not mention here the very strategic contribution brought in the defence of our case by respectful, attentive, and enlightened lawyers and jurists such as Antonio Lamer, then Chief Justice of Canada's Supreme Court; Louise Mandell; Peter Hutchins; Jacques Larochelle; Michel Pouliot; Alain Bissonnette; and many others.

CHAPTER FIVE

1 My first of these two was originally written for the collective *Indigena: Contemporary Native Perspectives*, published in 1992 by the Canadian Museum of Civilization (now renamed Canadian Museum of History).

2 This presentation also appears in French in Sioui, *Histories of Kanatha*, 353–62.

3 After the name *Huron* disparagingly given to the Wendat by the French, meaning uncouth and uncultured, and also referring to a hairstyle common among them reminiscent of a boar's bristle ("hure"), frequently used today among the youth under the name *mohawk*.

4 Jennings, *The Ambiguous Iroquois Empire* (New York: W.W. Norton, 1984), 99.

5 For more on this singular symbiotic political and cultural pre-European arrangement, readers may refer to the article by Kathryn Magee Labelle and myself, "The Algonquian-Wendat Alliance."

6 Beaver, in Wendat.

CHAPTER SIX

1 Cook, "Our Bodies, Ourselves," 6.
2 The term *gynecocentrism* (from the Greek *gynêkos*: the genitive form of the word *gynê*), which means woman, can be a substitute for *matricentrism*.
3 Eshibok-Trudeau, "Circular Vision," 20.
4 My readers may be interested in seeing the brief section on matriarchy in Sioui, *For an Amerindian Autohistory*, 15–19.
5 Ancestrally, the Wendat and all the Nadouek (Iroquoian) are among them.
6 I have no pretention that this word, which I have contrived, will find a place in any sort of literature. I simply use it here to help convey my idea.
7 There is saying among my people: A home that is under the man's rule is a dysfunctional home. "I am the boss, but my wife commands," used to say, jokingly and seriously, my father.
8 Spindler and Spindler, preface to Trigger, *The Huron*, vi.
9 Sioui, *Huron-Wendat*, 120.
10 Thwaites, *The Jesuit Relations*, 211–13.
11 Among present-day Hodenosaunee traditionalists, Clan Mothers still exercise their function of naming and, eventually, deposing chiefs. These women are the proprietors of the deer horns that Chiefs wear as part of their headgear as emblem of their position. After two warnings, a misguided, wayward Chief will get "dehorned" by his Clan Mothers.
12 Trigger, *The Huron*, 84.
13 Ibid., 81–2.
14 Sioui, *Huron-Wendat*, 131.

BIBLIOGRAPHY

Anderson, Karen Lee. "Huron Men and Huron Women: The
Effects of Demography, Kinship and the Social Division of
Labour on Male/Female Relationships among the 17th Century
Huron." PhD diss., University of Toronto, 1982.
– *Chain Her by One Foot: The Subjugation of Native Women in
Seventeenth-Century New France.* New York: Routledge, 1993.
Bacqueville de la Potherie, M. de (Claude-Charles Le Roy). *Histoire
de l'Amérique Septentrionale: divisée en quatre tomes.* Paris:
Brocas, 1753.
Barbeau, C. Marius. *Huron and Wyandot Mythology. Memoir 80.*
Ottawa: Department of Mines, Government Printing Bureau,
1915.
Batson, Laura. *Curvature: The Science and Soul of Nonlinearity.*
Ottawa: Blurb Incorporated, 2017.
Bruchac, Josepth. *Iroquois Stories. Part 2: Iroquois Women's
Stories.* Read by the author. Good Minds Records, 1988. Audio-
cassette and CD.
Bruchac, Joseph, and Michael J. Caduto. *Keepers of the Earth.* New
York: The Greenfield Review Press, New York, 1988.
Champlain, Samuel de. *The Works of Samuel de Champlain in Six
Volumes.* Edited by Henry P. Biggar. Toronto: Toronto University
Press, 1971.
Cartier, Jacques. *The Voyages of Jacques Cartier.* Translated and
edited by Henry P. Biggar. Ottawa: F.A. Acland, 1924.

Cook, Katsi. "Our Bodies, Our Selves: Information Inspires
    Action," 2016. http://www.ourbodiesourselves.org/about/
    contributors/katsi-cook/
Daveluy, Michelle, and Louis-Jacques Dorais, eds. *À la périphérie
    du centre: Les limites de l'hégémonie en anthropologie.*
    Montreal: Liber, 2009.
Dennis, Matthew J. "Cultivating a Landscape of Peace: The
    Iroquois New World." PhD diss., University of California
    (Berkeley), 1986.
Dobyns, Henry F., and William R. Swagerty. *Their Number Become
    Thinned: Native American Population Dynamics in Eastern
    North America.* Knoxville: University of Tennessee Press, 1983.
Eshkibok-Trudeau, Marie. "Circular Vision – Through Native
    Eyes." In *Voice of the Drum,* edited by Roger Neil. Brandon:
    Brandon University Press, 2000.
Fenton, William N. *The Roll Call of the Iroquois Chiefs: A Study
    of a Mnemonic Cane from the Six Nations Reserve.* 1950.
    Reprint, Washington: Smithsonian Institution, 1980.
French, Marilyn. *The War against Women.* New York: Summit
    Books, 1992.
Hammersmith, Bernice (Asisikoowatwaapiskosis). "Restoring
    Women's Value." *In Nation to Nation: Aboriginal Sovereignty
    and the Future of Canada,* edited by John Bird, Lorraine Land
    and Murray MacAdam. Toronto: Public Justice Resource Centre,
    2002.
Heidenreich, Conrad E. *Huronia: A History and Geography of the
    Huron Indians, 1600–1650.* Toronto: McClelland and Stewart,
    1971.
Ionita, Irina. *Un itinéraire de recherche en milieu autochtone au
    Canada. L'empathie dans tous ses états.* Paris: L'Hamattan, 2015.
Jennings, Francis. *The Ambiguous Iroquois Empire: The Covenant
    Chain Confederation of Indian Tribes with English Colonies
    from Its Beginnings to the Lancaster Treaty of 1744.* New York:
    W.W. Norton, 1984.
Kimmerer, Robin Wall. *Braiding Sweetgrass: Indigenous Wisdom,
    Scientific Knowledge and the Teachings of Plants.* Minneapolis:
    Milkweed Editions, 2013.

Kristof, Nicholas D., and Sheryl WuDunn. *Half the Sky: Turning Oppression into Opportunity for Women Worldwide*. New York: Vintage Books, 2009.

LaDuke, Winona. *Last Woman Standing*. St Paul: Voyageur Press, 1997.

Lafitau, Joseph-François. *Customs of the American Indians Compared with the Customs of Primitive Times*. Edited and translated by William N. Fenton and Elizabeth L. Moore. Toronto: Champlain Society, 2013.

Leduc, Timothy. *A Canadian Climate of Mind: Passages from Fur to Energy and Beyond*. Montreal and Kingston: McGill-Queen's University Press, 2016.

Lesage, L.N., N. Gupta, and G. Sioui. "Multidisciplinary Investigations into Huron-Wendat and St. Lawrence Iroquoian Connections." Neha Gupta and Louis Lesage, eds. *Ontario Archaeology* 96 (2016): 3–6.

Loyie, Larry. *Residential Schools, with the Words and Images of Survivors: A National History*. Brantford: Indigenous Education Press, 2016.

Maathai, Wangari. *Dirt! The Movie*. Directed by Bill Benenson and Gene Rosow. Common Ground Media, 2009.

MacKenzie, Sarah Emily. "White Settler Colonialism and Re(presentations) of Gendered Violence in Indigenous Women's Theatre." PhD diss., University of Ottawa, 2015.

Magee Labelle, Kathryn. *Dispersed but Not Destroyed – A History of the Seventeenth-Century Wendat People*. Vancouver: University of British Columbia Press, 2013.

Martin-Gropius-Bau. *Bundeskunsthalle. Auf den Spuren der Irokesen (On the Trails of the Iroquois)*. Berlin, 2013.

McMaster, Gerald and Lee Ann Martin. *Indigena: Contemporary Native Perspectives*. Ottawa: Canadian Museum of Civilization, 1992.

McMaster, Gerald, and Clifford T. Trafzer. *Native Universe: Voices of Indian America (Inaugural Book for the opening of the National Museum of the American Indian)*. Washington: The Smithsonian Institution, 2004.

Momaday, N. Scott. "Personal Reflections." In *The American*

Indian and the Problem of History. Edited by Calvin Martin. New York: Oxford University Press, 1987.

– *The House Made of Dawn.* New York: Harper Collins Publishers, 1966.

Murray, General James. "Report to His Britannick Majesty, June 5th, 1762." Canadian Archives: Documents Relating to the Constitutional History of Canada. Sessional Papers no. 18. Edited by Adam Short and Arthur Doughty (Ottawa 1907).

Nabigon, Herbert. *The Hollow Tree: Fighting Addiction with Traditional Native Healing.* Montreal and Kinston: McGill-Queen's University Press, 2006.

Ouellet, Réal, ed. *Sur Lahontan.* Quebec: L'Hêtrière, 1983.

Neil, Roger, ed. *Voice of the Drum.* Brandon: Kingfisher Publications, 2000.

Peace, Thomas, and Kathryn Magee Labelle. *From Huronia to Wendakes: Adversity, Migrations and Resilience.* Norman: University of Oklahoma Press, 2016.

Reichel-Dolmatoff, Gerardo. *Indios de Colombia: Momentos Vividos, Mundos Concebidos.* Bogotá: Villegas Editores, 1991.

Rice, Bryan. *The Rotinonshonni: A Traditional Iroquoian History through the Eyes of Teharonhia:wako and Sawiskera.* Syracuse: Syracuse University Press, 2013.

Santiemma, Adriano. *Viaggio sul Sentiero Irochese.* Roma : Bulzoni Editore, 1998.

– *L'Unione dei Cinquanta Cieli di Iroquoia.* Roma: Bulzoni Editore, 1998.

Sioui, Éléonore Tecumseh. "A Huron-Wyandot Woman's Life Story: The Realization of an Impossible Dream." PhD diss. Cincinnati, The Union Institute, 1989.

Sioui, Georges. *For an Amerindian Autohistory: Essay on the Foundation of a Social Ethics.* Montreal and Kingston: McGill-Queen's University Press (translated from the French), 1992.

– *Huron-Wendat: The Heritage of the Circle.* Vancouver: UBC Press (translated from the French), 1999.

– *Histories of Kanatha Seen and Told/Histoires de Kanatha vues et racontées.* Ottawa: University of Ottawa Press, 2008.

– *Seawi.* New Orleans: Dialogos/Lavender Ink Press, 2013.

– "Americity: The Integration of the Americas through Their Indigenous Cosmologies." *The Canadian Journal of Native Studies* 36, no. 1 (2016): 225–30.

Sioui, Georges, and Kathryn Magee Labelle. "The Algonquian-Wendat Alliance. A Case Study of Circular-Thinking Societies." *The Canadian Journal of Native Studies* 34, no. 1 (2014): 171–83.

Sioui Labelle, René, dir. *Kanata: The Legacy of the Children of Aataentsic*. Canada: National Film Board of Canada, 1999.

Sioui, Mabel (Huron-Wendat Elder). "History of Canada: History of Her Huron People." In the author's possession.

Sioui, Miguel Paul. "Investigating the Current State of a Yucatec Maya Community's Land Use Knowledges and Their Potential to 'Indigenize' Mainstream Environmental Thinking." PhD diss., University of Carleton, 2018.

Steckley, John. *Words of the Huron*. Waterloo: Wilfrid Laurier University Press, 2007.

Stirbys, Cynthia Darlene. "Potentializing Wellness through the Stories of Female Survivors of Indian Residential Schools: A Grounded Theory Study." PhD diss., University of Ottawa, 2015.

Thwaites, Ruben Gold, ed. *The Jesuit Relations and Allied Documents, 1600–1791*. 73 vols. Cleveland: Burrows, 1898.

Trigger, Bruce G. *The Children of Aataentsic. A History of the Huron People to 1650*. 2nd ed. Montreal and Kingston: McGill-Queen's University Press, 1987.

– *The Huron: Farmers of the North*. 2nd ed. New York: Holt, Rinehart and Winston, 1990.